IN SEARCH OF UNKNOWN BRITAIN

By the same author

FICTION

Snake in the Grass
A Moment in Time
Journey to a High Mountain
Woman Returning
Deep Is the Night
Night in Babylon
Summer at the Castle
Action of the Tiger
Memoirs of a Cross-eyed Man
Conversations with a Witch
The Affair in Arcady
A Sound of Trumpets
A Man and His Journey
You with the Roses – What are you Selling?
The Sun-Gazers

NON-FICTION

Understanding the English
General George S. Patton
The Ancient Way
Looking at Italy
The Great Sahara
Lost Worlds of Africa
Desert Pilgrimage
By the Waters of Babylon
The Search for the Etruscans
The French Foreign Legion
The Search for Lost Worlds
Samarkand and Beyond
The Search for Lost Cities

Mithras, the Persian god whose cult once rivalled Christianity, had five known shrines in Roman Britain. The most splendid was located in London where this head of the god in his Phrygian cap was found in the ruins of his temple.

IN SEARCH OF UNKNOWN BRITAIN

James Wellard

Constable . London

First published in Great Britain 1983
by Constable and Company Limited
10 Orange Street London WC2H 7EG

ISBN 0 09 463610 9
Set in Linotron Baskerville 11pt by
Rowland Phototypesetting Limited
Bury St Edmunds, Suffolk
Printed in Great Britain by
St Edmundsbury Press
Bury St Edmunds, Suffolk

CONTENTS

Acknowledgements xv
Introduction xvii

1 THE DISCOVERY OF THE PRETANIC ISLES 1
Hengistbury Head (South Dorset): An Iron Age Trading Post 12
Carn Brea (Cornwall): an Iron Age Hill Fort 14
Jarlshof (Shetland): an Iron Age Farmstead 16

2 THE PHOENICIANS IN BRITAIN 20
St Michael's Mount (Cornwall): a Phoenician Port? 31
The Scilly Islands: the Cassiterides? 33
Truro (Cornwall): the Museum 36

3 BRITANNIA FELIX 40
Colchester (Essex): the First Romano-British City 55
Portchester (Hampshire): a Roman Naval Station 60
Dolaucothi (Carmarthenshire, Wales): a Roman Gold Mine 62

4 GODS AND GHOSTS: THE RELIGIONS OF ROMAN BRITAIN 66
Bath (Avon): the Temple of Sulis 81
London: the Temple of Mithras 84
Lullingstone (Kent): the Christian Chapel 87

5 THE GROANS OF THE BRITONS 91
Vercovicium – Housesteads (Cumbria): a Roman Fort 100
Candida Casa (Wigtown, Scotland) *Fifth Century Monasteries* 103
Llantwit Major (Glamorgan, Wales) 105
Tintagel (Cornwall) 107

6 HEATHEN KINGS AND CHRISTIAN SAINTS 110
Canterbury (Kent): the Cradle of British Christianity 126
Sutton Hoo (Suffolk): the Last of the Pagan Tombs 128
Whitby (Yorkshire): the Abbess and the Poet 133

7 OUT OF THE DARKNESS 137
Offa's Dyke: from the Irish Sea to the Bristol Channel 151
York: the Danish Kingdom, AD 866–1066 153
Bosham (Sussex): Remembrances of Saxon England 157

Epilogue 161
Bibliography 167
Index 177

LIST OF ILLUSTRATIONS

Mithras, the Persian god whose cult once rivalled Christianity, had five known shrines in Roman Britain, of which little remains. The most splendid was located in London where this head of the god in his Phrygian cap was found in the ruins of his temple. (*Courtesy Museum of London*) *frontispiece*

Map of Britain showing the sites mentioned xvi

A fifteenth-century map based on the *Geography* of Ptolemy. The ancient Greeks' knowledge of the 'Pretanic Isles' was largely derived from an account of a voyage to northern Europe by the explorer Pytheas. (*Courtesy British Museum*) xix

Map showing Hengistbury Head in relation to trading routes, and the exports and imports handled there. 12

Prehistoric Britain, particularly the south and west, was notable for its hillforts, of which Maiden Castle in Dorset is the best preserved. (*Courtesy Aerofilms*) 15

The fortress-farmhouse of Jarlshof was the 'capital' of Stone Age immigrants who arrived in the Shetlands over 3000 years ago. The site they selected was occupied almost continuously until modern times. (*Courtesy Scottish Tourist Board*) 17

St Michael's Mount, to-day a tourist resort, was probably the port of the Phoenician fleet which visited Cornwall 2500 years ago to barter for tin. The island on which the abbey now stands was known to the Romans as Ictis. (*Courtesy British Tourist Authority*) 32

Tresco, Scilly, is thought by some historians to be one of the Cassiterides, or Tin Islands, mentioned by Herodotus. A prehistoric chambered tomb, one of 61 discovered in the Scillies, was found here. Cromwell's Castle, the tower in the photograph, is part of the island's 3000-year history. (*Courtesy English Tourist Board*) 35

Two of the artefacts now in the Truro Museum, an ingot of tin weighing 158 lbs, and the statuette of a bronze bull, were believed by the old antiquaries to be of Phoenician provenance. The ingot is certainly pre-Roman, the bull probably Egyptian. (*Courtesy Truro Museum*) 37

The mosaic of a North African villa, from the Bardo Museum, Tunis, illustrates the architecture of a rich landowner's farmhouse of the type built all over southern Britain during the Roman occupation. (*Courtesy Bardo Museum*) 41

The Roman centurion, Marcus Favonius Facilis, was buried at Colchester, or, as he would have called it, Colonia Claudia Victricensis. He is a personification of the legions which conquered Britain. (*Courtesy Colchester Museum*) 57

To defend the pirate-infested seas around the British Isles, the Romans created a special fleet, the *classis britannica*, and built a chain of naval stations along the eastern, southern, and western coasts. The largest of these fortified harbours was Portus Adurni, to-day Portchester Castle. 61

The Romans burrowed deep into the Welsh hillside at Dolaucothi mining for gold. Little remains to be seen of their extensive workings except for entrances to the galleries, traces of aqueducts, and water tanks. The photograph shows one of the entrances to the Romans' mine at Dolaucothi. (*Courtesy Dr Roger Wilson*) 63

The shrines of the Mother goddesses (the Matres) were found all over Celtic Europe. This example of Romano-British sculpture shows the deities, some with their offerings of fruit, and one with a baby. (*Courtesy Museum of London*) 67

Bronze statuettes of Venus were popular as ornaments throughout the Roman provinces; but the existence of this example from Verulamium (St Albans) does not mean that the cult of the goddess was observed in Britain. (*Courtesy Museum of St Albans*) 68

Stonehenge has long been associated with Druidic rituals. Even to-day, votaries of the ancient British priesthood come to this prehistoric monument on the summer solstice to see the sun rise. (*Courtesy Aerofilms*) 73

The abbey seen behind the Great Bath reminds us that Aquae Sulis was also a religious centre in Roman times, with a temple dedicated to the Celtic goddess Sul, identified with Minerva. (*Courtesy English Tourist Board*) 82

Mithras, worshipped throughout the Roman Empire principally by army officers and wealthy merchants, sacrifices a bull in the ceremony known as the *taurobolium*. Penitents were bespattered with the bull's blood in a form of baptism which gave the promise of eternal life. (*Courtesy Museum of London*) 85

Six *orantes*, or Christian worshippers with hands raised in prayer, were painted on the wall of the Christian chapel in a Roman villa at Lullingstone in Kent. (*Courtesy British Museum*) 88

The fort of Vercovicium (Housesteads) about midway along Hadrian's Wall is an excellent example of Roman military architecture. Facilities included a hospital, baths, special quarters for officers, barracks for the men, and a latrine, shown here. (*Courtesy Roger Wilson*) 100

Drawing showing the main features of Hadrian's Wall. The Wall was commissioned by Emperor Hadrian in 122 to act as a frontier between the barbarian tribes of northern England and their potential allies in southern Scotland. Stretching from coast to coast, it required 15,000 auxiliaries to man its forts, milecastles, and look-out turrets. 101

The stone walls in this photograph of Tintagel in Cornwall are said to demarcate the cells of the nuns who occupied a monastery established here in the fifth century. The site was originally the hermitage of St Gwen, Celtic saint and legendary mother of St David. (*Courtesy British Tourist Authority*) 108

The bronze stag surmounted the sceptre of the East Anglian king Raedwald whose warship, but not his body, was entombed at Sutton Hoo. Excavations of the burial mound yielded the richest haul of Anglo-Saxon treasures in the annals of archaeology. (*Courtesy British Museum*) 129

An old photograph shows the excavation of the Sutton Hoo warship. (*Courtesy British Museum*) 130

The ruins of the abbey of Whitby, built in 1078 on the site of the double monastery of St Hilda. This holy place was the venue of the Synod of Whitby presided over by King Oswy of Northumbria in AD 664. The cell of Caedmon, the first English poet, is said to lie beneath the crypt of the ruined abbey. (*Courtesy British Tourist Authority*) 135

King Alfred, the first 'king of the English' and our only monarch to be called 'The Great', stands overlooking the market square at Wantage, Oxfordshire, where he was said to have been born in AD 849. (*Courtesy English Tourist Board*) 142

Offa's Dyke, named after the eighth-century king of Mercia who built it, runs some 149 miles in a north-south direction from the Irish Sea to the Bristol Channel. It was intended to form a frontier between Anglo-Saxon England and British Wales. What remains of part of this earth-wall can be seen in this aerial photograph as a white line. (*Courtesy Aerofilms*) 152

A leather shoe, a sock, and a storage jar were a few of the finds of recent excavations of Viking York. Such humble articles of everyday life tell historians a great deal about the Danish colony of Jervik, founded in 866 and lasting about 200 years. (*Courtesy York Archaelogical Trust*) 154

The Bayeux Tapestry's picture of Bosham Church as it looked in 1064. King Harold is shown entering the church before embarking for Normandy. The chancel arch survives in its original Saxon form. (*Below*) Harold feasts in a mansion which probably belonged to King Canute whose little daughter, drowned in a nearby creek, is said to be buried in Bosham Church. (*Courtesy Victoria and Albert Museum and Phaidon Press*) 158

A page from the Domesday Book with the entry for the Manor of Chelsea, whose total value is assessed at £9. (*Courtesy British Museum*) 163

William Camden (1551–1623), the English antiquary and author of *Britania*, who set out in 1580 'to acquaint the world with the ancient state of Britain'. (*Courtesy National Portrait Gallery, London*) 166

ACKNOWLEDGMENTS

I would like to thank the many officials of museums and historic monuments I visited in the course of my travels for their help and advice. I am also indebted to the authors of the old guide books, and especially to the archaeologists who excavated at remote sites in the British Isles. Their reports will be found in the Bibliography at the end of this book. This long list of books also includes the writings of the old antiquaries who described many historic places since obliterated or destroyed within the last hundred years. Their books are, alas! now out of print, and to-day's 'explorer' of unknown Britain will only be able to consult most of them in one of the great national libraries – in my case, the British Library. I now record my thanks to the Superintendent and Staff of the British Museum Reading Room for their help and cooperation.

Special thanks to the English Tourist Board which gave me free access to their photo library; to Moira Johnston who edited the typescript for the press; to Elfreda Powell, a director of Constable, who coordinated publication; to Ivor Kamlish who worked with us in the preparation of the maps; and to Barbara Nelson-Smith who undertook the onerous job of reading and typing my manuscript.

James Wellard
London, 1983

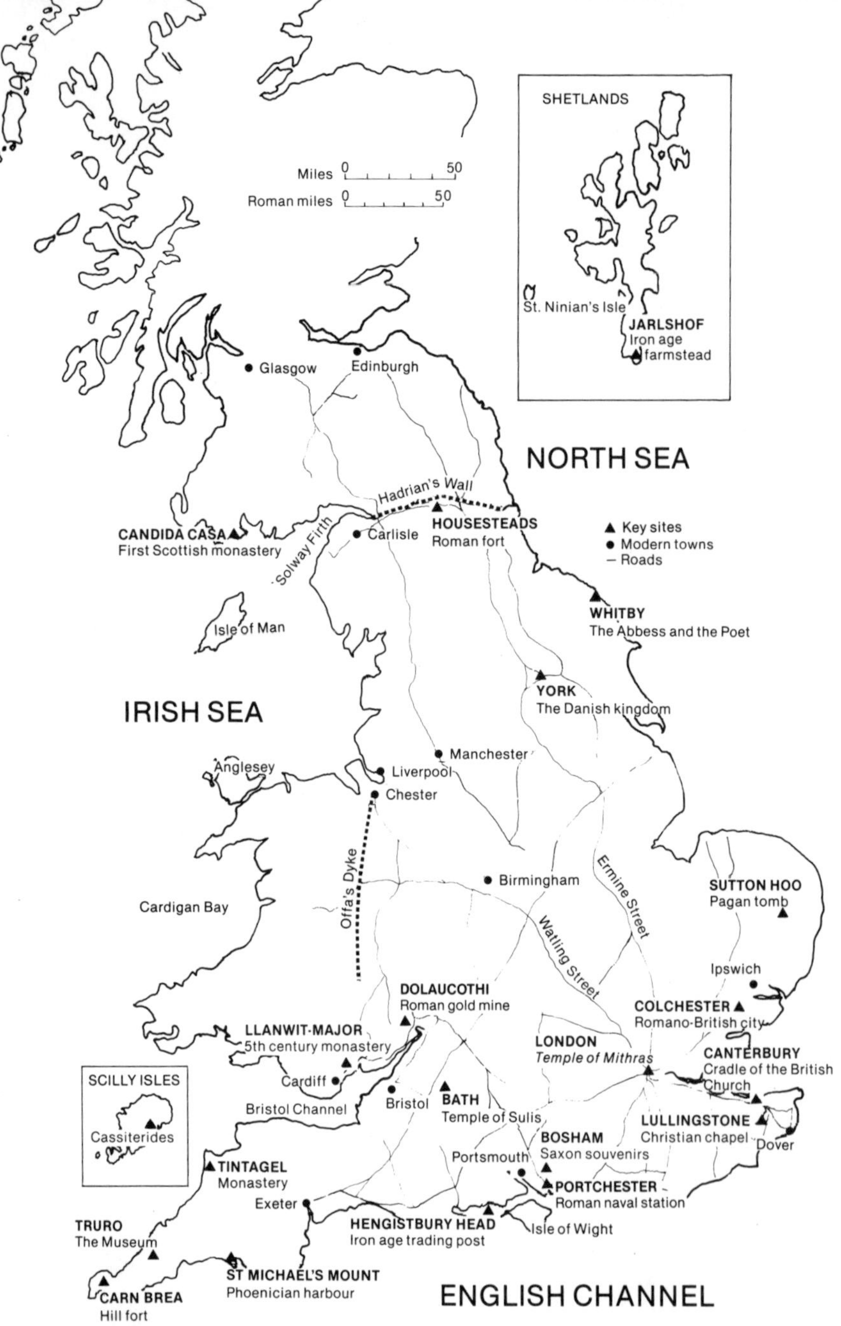

1 Map of Britain showing the sites mentioned

INTRODUCTION

In 1536, John Leland, the antiquary, set out on a tour of England to search for 'the secrets of antiquity'. He intended to write a description of his findings in sixty-five volumes after visiting 'every bay, river, lake, mountain, valley, moor, heath, wood, city, castle, manor house, monastery, and college in the land'.[1] For a scholar who had spent most of his life in university libraries, the undertaking of a journey of thousands of miles riding or walking every mile of the way may seem curious to modern travellers who cross continents without ever setting a foot to the ground. But such an enterprise did not daunt a sixteenth-century Englishman who could write a poem in Latin on how to capture and tame a squirrel and, with equal facility, ditties to be sung to Ann Boleyn at her coronation.

Henry VIII appointed John Leland Royal Antiquary in 1533 and sent him off on a tour which was to last for nearly ten years. At the end of it, Leland's claim to have actually visited every bay, river, lake, et cetera is figuratively justified by the very size of his report, appropriately entitled *The Laboryouse Journey And Serche by John Lelande For Englandes Antiquitees*, in which he carefully notes every object of interest pertaining to the thousands of places he visited. He is not, alas! a gossipy writer and seldom gives us a glimpse of the people he met on the road, although he was observant enough to describe boys diving for coins in the Roman piscina at Bath; but he remains more of a topographer than a travel-writer, and his massive book is of interest nowadays primarily to historians and geographers.

As regards my own 'Serche', I am not, of course, trying to

[1] *The Itinerary of John Leland*. London: Centaur Press, 1964. Vol. i, p. xli.

emulate a man who compared himself with Virgil and Catullus:

Mantua Virgilium genuit, Verona Catullum,
Patria Londinum est urbs generosa mihi.

Nor can I expect to rival Leland's successor, William Camden, who undertook the same grand tour in 1570, thereby leaving himself open to the accusation of 'feathering his own nest with Leland's plumes'. The charge is manifestly unfair. Camden prepared himself much more thoroughly for his task than Leland by teaching himself Welsh and Anglo-Saxon in order to read the manuscripts he expected to find in the ruined monasteries, ruined by Leland's patron, Henry VIII. Many of these treasures had been carried off by Germans who 'perceiving our negligence do daily send young scholars hither that spoileth manuscripts by cutting them out, returning home and putting them abroad as monuments of their own country.'[2]

In Search of Unknown Britain resembles the 'laboryouse journeys' of my Tudor predecessors in that, like them, I have been looking at my country from the viewpoint of an 'explorer', not as the writer of another guidebook – and certainly not of another history text book. I have tried to see Britain with something of the curiosity I experienced on my expeditions in Africa where the oases in the sand seas of the Central Sahara, for instance, were as strange and fascinating to me as the Iron Age Settlements of 'The Pretanic Isles' must have been to the Greek navigator Pytheas. At the same time, I realize that it is no longer possible to see Britain as Leland or Camden saw it, let alone Pytheas. Our nation with its sprawling cities and dense population seems to have no connection whatsoever with a country once infested with wolves and bears, as in Roman times, or swarming with monks and hermits, as in the age of the Celtic saints. But my object was to search out as far as I could from contemporary accounts what remained of these strange

[2] William Huddesford, *The Life of John Leland, the Antiquary*. Oxford: Clarendon Press, 1772. Vol. i, p. 85.

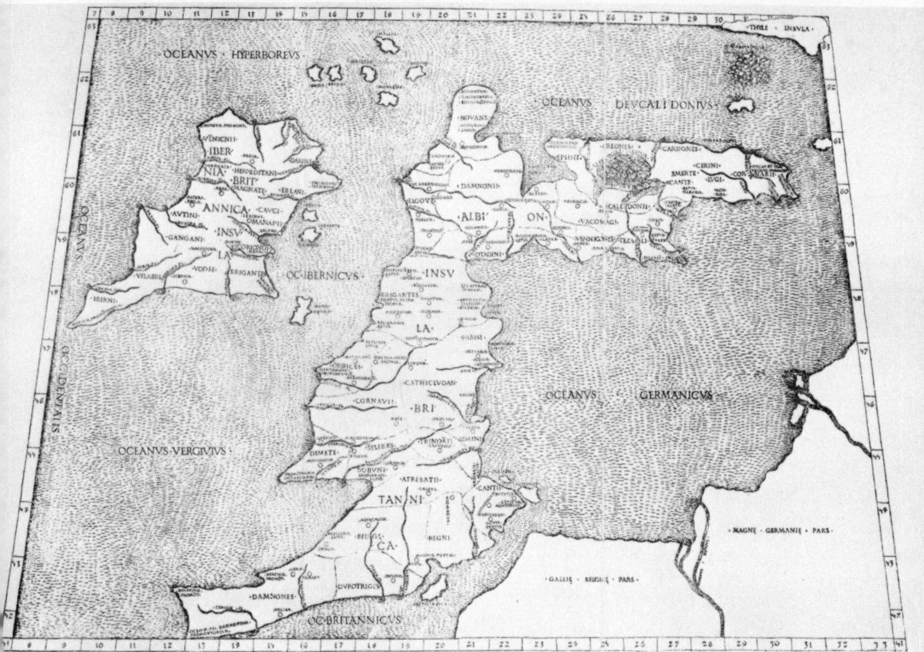

2 A fifteenth-century map based on the *Geography* of Ptolemy. The ancient Greeks' knowledge of the 'Pretanic Isles' was largely derived from an account of a voyage to northern Europe by the explorer Pytheas.

and interesting periods and then to suggest where the traveller with an exploring bent could go to get a glimpse of his ancestors' homeland.

But is there anything left to explore? Surprisingly, the answer is yes, despite the impression one gets, particularly in our cities, that the planners have demolished so much of our architectural heritage that there is very little worthwhile left to see. Saxon churches have been destroyed, mediaeval houses torn down, Georgian squares 'modernized', usually to make way for office blocks or road junctions. But once away from the centres frequented by the weekend motorist, the traveller can still find relics of almost every period – even of prehistoric Britain, especially if he is prepared to tramp across a muddy field or two. A glance at the *Ordnance Survey of Ancient Britain*, the atlas of the major visible antiquities older than AD 1066, will show how much there is left to see of the Britain of Pytheas and the Phoenicians. It will show, too, that Stonehenge is by no means the only surviving Iron Age monument. A vast complex of pre-Roman settlements – cliff castles, earthworks, and underground refuges – still await the student of prehistory, if he has the enthusiasm and imagination to explore them.

Hence it is to places like Carn Brea, the great hill fortress in north-west Cornwall, rather than to Stonehenge that the reader of *In Search of Unknown Britain* will be directed. Carn Brea, in turn, with its hut village inside the fortress walls, may have been occupied by the tin miners of the Phoenician period when St Michael's Mount was the principal Phoenician emporium in Britain. If so, what evidence can we find for the visitations of these old seafarers? And where do we go to find clues of their presence? So, too, Roman Britain – in a way the most curious and exciting of our several Britains – is sought out not just by a visit to the traditional sites – Hadrian's Wall or Verulamium – but by a journey to the Welsh mountains where the vestiges of a gold mine at Dolaucothi in Carmarthenshire evoke the world of industry and trade in these islands during the third and fourth centuries AD.

I have concluded *In Search of Unknown Britain* with the Dark Ages whose termination can arbitrarily be identified with the Norman Conquest for reasons I state in the Epilogue. From 1086 onwards, Britain ceases to be 'unknown' in the sense that, say, Hengistbury Head, the Iron Age settlement on the Dorset coast, is unknown, or a buried Roman city like Calleva Atrebatum (Silchester) – unknown because so foreign to the twentieth-century English scene. The Domesday Book of 1086 with its mass of social and economic data – facts and figures which make a modern census look almost superficial – foreshadows the United Kingdom we recognize to-day: that is, a nation in which every one of us is, or is supposed to be, accounted for in the archives of government, just as the 'three slaves' listed in the Domesday Book Survey of Chelsea were accounted for in our first national census of 1086.[3]

It will be noted that each chapter deals with an historical period, and is divided into two parts. The first part aims to present an eyewitness account of the period, derived as far as possible from contemporary documents. The second part suggests ideas for visiting historic sites chosen to illustrate the theories I have put forward in the first part and sometimes recommended for their scenic as well as their archaeological interest. The reader who opts to explore some of these sites should be warned that the relics of our early history are usually photogenically very disappointing. They are often neglected piles of rubble, so that a real effort of the imagination is needed to see them as temples, palaces, monasteries, and homesteads. In contrast, it is hoped that those readers who prefer to do their exploring from the comfort of an armchair will find the maps and illustrations evocative enough for them to complete their own journey into the past.

[3] See p. 162.

[1]

THE DISCOVERY OF THE PRETANIC ISLES

Beyond the Pillars of Hercules the Ocean flows around the Earth. In this Ocean are two very large islands called the Pretanic Isles: one is Albion, the other Ierne.

Pseudo-Aristotle, *On the Cosmos*

Seated on straw around low tables, stuffing food into their mouths with their fingers, and washing everything down with draughts of beer from earthenware pots, the British gentry around the fourth century BC liked to enliven their festivities with a brawl which often ended with the death of one of the contestants. The women were as bellicose as the men: in the event of a fight, the ladies would appear on the scene, pitching in with hair streaming and punching and kicking 'with the force of a catapult'.[1] The Greek traveller who reported these goings-on detected little difference from the behaviour or the appearance of the males and females. 'Unisex' seems to him to have been the quality most typical of barbarians, for men and women in the Celtic lands, which included Britain at this time, looked and dressed alike: both sexes wore a blouse with sleeves, in some cases a belt, trousers fitted close to the ankle, and a tartan cape fastened at the shoulder with a brooch. Both sexes liked jewellery – collars and torques, necklaces and bracelets, strings of beads, and rings on all their fingers. They wore their hair hanging down their backs 'like a horse's mane'. As in all primitive societies, women were excluded from the banquets, which were orgies of eating and drinking, the food consisting

[1] *Posidonius. 1. The Fragments.* Edited by L. Edelstein and I. G. Kidd. Cambridge: University Press, 1972. p. 84.

chiefly of roasted or boiled meats, washed down with cups of beer carried from guest to guest by boys. The diners sucked in their drink by small mouthfuls, filtering the beer through their long moustaches. The minstrels sang, the harpers twanged their harps, and the company either got comatose or belligerent. In the latter case, a fight to the death would be regarded by those who could still sit upright (and possibly by the ladies who took part) as a worth-while evening's entertainment.

We are indebted for this information to a Greek traveller called Posidonius of Apames who around 100 BC visited Gaul where he was the guest of various tribal chieftains. What he described could equally well have applied to the Britons across the Channel, except that Britain at that time was still *terra incognita*, whose existence was known only to a few geographers in the academies of Alexandria and Rome under the name of 'The Pretanic Isles'.

Who was the explorer who first gave this name to our nation?[2] What prompted him to venture outside the Pillars of Hercules, those Gates which shut off the familiar world of the Mediterranean from the mysterious ocean-river which, according to the ancient and, indeed, mediaeval geographers, flowed ceaselessly round the Earth? Was he a Phoenician, Carthaginian, or a Tartessian sea-captain who brought from thence gold and tin and amber to the kingdoms of the Middle East? We shall never know the answers to such questions, but we have a few clues as to who discovered these islands and what the first explorers saw when they got here.

Even to-day the sailor who approaches the English coast from the continent of Europe is viewing the same headlands which the first visitors from the Mediterranean sighted three, perhaps even four, thousand years ago. If you sail north-north-east from Cap de la Hague in a small boat, you will glimpse after a day and a night at sea the chalk cliffs and green hills of the Isle of Wight; and if you set your course westwards instead,

[2] The name makes its first appearance in the *History* of Timaeus (*c* 356–260 BC) as νηςοι πρετανικαι.

you will make a landfall off Hengistbury Head, whose Bronze Age hillfort was a landmark for the Phoenician shipmaster, and whose sheltered lagoon was a harbour for his galley. You have discovered anew that country which Virgil declared lay 'beyond the frontiers of the world'.

We shall never know where the Greek explorer Pytheas, who wrote the first account of these islands, made his actual landfall, but as soon as he sighted the British coast, he would have discovered that there were very few anchorages suitable for his purpose. It was no use landing where there was no sign of human habitation, for the explorer had made his voyage to find out what were the possibilities of a profitable trade with the barbarians of northern Europe. However, it was easy enough to tell whether or not there was a settlement. If a likely-looking inlet revealed an expanse of mud flats at low tide with trees coming right down to the water's edge, no one would be living in such a place. Why? Because it was unsuitable and dangerous: crops were difficult to cultivate; domestic animals were preyed on by wild beasts; people were attacked by bears and wolves; and the forest stretched away unbroken into an unknown interior where no one ventured.

If, in contrast, the mariners coasting along the beaches and cliffs spied an open space of downs or heath, they would be pretty certain of spotting signs of human activity – smoke rising from fires, sheep and goats grazing on the sides of grassy hills, dogs barking, and then people standing on the shore, ready either to welcome them as friendly traders or to flee from them as enemies. Captain Cook had exactly the same reception on his voyages to Australia.

On landing, Pytheas and his companions would be cautiously welcomed by the locals, who would take them to the residence of the chieftain. The Britons lived in huts inside defensive enclosures and sometimes in lake villages on artificial mounds. The explorer would have seen many of these settlements on his voyage along the southern and western coasts, for almost every headland had its hillfort or cliff castle, scores of which still survive. They served not only as strongholds, but also as villages, for many of them, like Maiden Castle in Dorset, enclosed enough land to make the community inside self-sufficient and relatively secure. Others, like the trading posts at Hengistbury Head and St Michael's Mount, were free ports for international shipping.

But Pytheas knew nothing of this when he set sail from Marseilles in 325 BC. Indeed, all that his contemporaries seem to have known of northern Europe was a hodge-podge of myths going back to the time of Homer and those legendary Cimmerians who lived in a land 'where the paths of day and night lie close together'. The thought of the sunless days and long nights of those regions on the edge of the Ocean and the tales of the fearful sea-monsters which inhabited that Ocean appalled the Greek seamen who were seldom out of sight of land in the Mediterranean. On the other hand, talk of the Pillars of Hercules being the divinely appointed terminus of sea-travel, of a circumambient river called Ocean, of sea-monsters and navigational hazards, never seems to have deterred the Phoenicians who had been passing through the Pillars from the time of King Solomon (3000 BC) when their ships had reached lands unknown to the other Mediterranean nations. The Phoenicians, and after them the Carthaginians, were not telling their commercial rivals the secrets of their trade routes; and that is why the Greek geographers were almost completely in the dark as to the whereabouts of the 'Pretanic Isles'. The only source of information available was the narrative of Pytheas who published a book sometime in the fourth century BC claiming that he had actually sailed round and walked about these islands, a claim which the savants back in Alexandria, the centre of astronomical and geographical sciences, refused to believe, dismissing the explorer as an outright impostor. As a result, the cartographers, even Ptolemy, the greatest of them, never really solved the 'problem' of Britain, and the general ignorance was such that even after *Britannia* was a province of the Roman Empire, the learned and much-travelled Jewish historian

Josephus was still referring to it in AD 75 as 'a world beyond the Ocean'.

There were two reasons for this ignorance concerning Britain and, for that matter, of the whole of northern Europe. The first was a hard core of curious legends and fanciful myths about the undiscovered regions of the world which must have made an intelligent Athenian, for instance, sceptical about the latest reports from 'Outer Space'. Our Athenian – indeed, any educated Greek whether in the mother-country or one of the cities of the Hellenic world – had heard from his infancy stories of the Hyperboreans who lived at the back of the north wind in a land of perpetual sunshine where the swans sang like nightingales. He knew all about one-footed men, Germans with monstrous ears that flapped as they ran, cannibals that ate their mothers, men whose heads grew beneath their shoulders, and so on. These aberrations were the flying saucers, Loch Ness Monsters, and Bermuda Triangles of the fourth century BC. And so when a genuine explorer, like Pytheas, returned from his expedition to the 'New World' with an account of what he had seen, he was greeted with derision by academicians who had had enough of one-footed, flapping-eared men and like absurdities. Thus it was that the Britain discovered by Pytheas was really lost again to the world for three centuries, until 55 BC when Julius Caesar, in a sense, re-discovered it, just as Greenland vanished from the scene for the three hundred years between 1410 when the Norse settlements became extinct and 1721 when the Danish missionaries re-settled that land.

The other, and possibly more basic, reason for ignorance was the disdain educated Greeks and Romans felt towards peoples who lived beyond the cultural frontiers of the Mediterranean, peoples whom they regarded as either barbarians or savages. This is how Strabo at the beginning of our era describes the Irish, for instance: 'They are cannibals and coarse feeders, and think it decent to eat up their dead parents and to have open intercourse with women, even their mothers and sisters.' The charge of having women in common was not, of course, a serious one, since the Greeks and Romans assumed that all primitive people were polygamous, as Caesar remarked of the Britons. Cannibalism, on the other hand, was particularly repugnant to civilized people, which explains why the Romans regarded with abhorrence religious fraternities like the Druids and the Christians, both of whom were suspected of anthropophagism.

Even more significant than these moral considerations was the unimportance economically of these islands to the ancient world. Caesar had to admit that the place was hardly worth the effort of conquest, since apart from some gold, silver, iron, hides, slaves, and hunting dogs, there was little of value to exploit and export. So even the first real on-the-spot explorations of the country added little to the sum of knowledge, which may explain why the Romans again lost interest, at least for the next century, in a land which lay 'beyond the frontiers of the world'.

One can see the extent of their ignorance from the maps of the time. The cartographers obviously still had no idea of the size, shape, or geography of these islands and continued to place them as if lying on an east-west axis instead of north-south: that is, turning the land ninety degrees on its side. Ptolemy's map of Europe, drawn up around 150 AD, affords the most striking example of the defects which characterize the work of the ancient geographers: and his delineation of the Pretanic Isles, including Ivernia (Ireland), Thule (the Shetlands) and Orcades (Orkneys), is a complete distortion of their actual shape and location. So, too, knowledge of the inhabitants was either erroneous or quasi-legendary, even though by AD 84 almost the entire country had been at least reconnoitred by military expeditions and circumnavigated by the Roman fleet. From what he had read in books, the average Italian would have described the Britons as tall, hairy, bandy-legged creatures, badly proportioned physically, uncouth in their habits, knowing little of gardening and any form of animal husbandry, content to live in conditions of uncivilized squalor, and so ignorant they didn't even know how to make cheese! For so said the experts. In short, the Romans and all the Romanized people of the Mediterranean regarded the Britons very much as an eighteenth-century Englishman would have regarded the inhabitants of Tierra del Fuego.

It is this ignorance of the peoples of northern Europe which sets aside the Massiliot navigator Pytheas as one of the great explorers of history, a coequal of Columbus, Vasco da Gama, and James Cook. Pytheas obviously had the same qualities as these famous captains – the seamanship, navigational skill, fortitude, and a truly scientific mind. Even so, it is extremely unlikely that the Greek sailor set out on his voyage with the sole intention of discovering some distant land, since there was very little interest in exploration for its own sake in the fourth century BC. Pytheas must, then, have undertaken this extremely dangerous journey for the same reason that sea-captains from the time of Prince Henry the Navigator up to the Elizabethan age set out to reach unknown lands across unchartered seas. They were looking for treasure and trade.

He sailed probably with a squadron of two or three ships provided by the merchants of Marseilles, first heading west along the French coast and then south past Spain to the Pillars of Hercules. Once beyond the Straits, he progressed northwards up the Iberian coast as far as Cape St Vincent, the Sacred Promontory of the classical geographers who considered this headland to be the most westerly point of continental Europe, which it is not. As soon as Pytheas had crossed the Bay of Biscay he reported that another headland projected out still farther into the Atlantic, a cape he called Calbion, which he calculated was 2000 *stadia* (200 miles) *west* of the Sacred Promontory. He was badly out in his calculations here, since Calbion, which we assume to be Ushant, lies 230 miles *east* of Cape St Vincent. What probably happened is that he had been swept westwards by the tides and winds while heading north across the Bay of Biscay.

His navigational errors, like all the miscalculations of classical geographers, are understandable. To begin with, the old cartographers were up against insurmountable difficulties in trying to fix precise positions by latitude and longitude, let alone in accurately charting such geophysical features as coasts, hills, mountain ranges, and rivers. All the locations they assigned to places are really inspired guesses; and in Pytheas's case the problems of estimating distances were enormous. His ships, square-rigged and steered by an oar, were almost unmanoeuvrable except with winds abaft the beam. One recalls how St Paul's ship was quite unable to claw off a lee coast when sailing past Malta, even with a beam wind, which a modern yachtsman would call a 'soldier's wind' on account of the ease with which a Bermuda-rigged vessel can be steered on this point of sailing. Anyone who has cruised along the coasts of Britain can imagine the difficulties and dangers the old seamen encountered in their cumbersome vessels; and one wonders how Pytheas managed to keep any sort of precise log as he worked his ships round the headlands of St Alban, Portland Bill, and the Lizard against the south-west winds, though as an experienced mariner, he must quickly have learnt how to use the tides. He also had the advantage of a beamy though shallow hull, so that his boat or boats rode fairly comfortably in a swell, were easy to row, and could be safely beached.

His principal disadvantage was the absence of a compass, without which navigation to-day seems inconceivable, though the instrument was not in general use on the high seas until seven hundred years ago when the Italians seem to have been the first to rely on it for their navigation. But the lack of this wonderful aid does not seem to have handicapped maritime peoples anywhere in the world, and would certainly not have deterred Pytheas who sailed, like all his forebears, by the natural signs and portents available to the observant mariner. He used the heavenly bodies to give him his bearings, while making an educated guess at distance covered (depending on the strength of the wind and tide), direction sailed, leeway and so forth. Even so, the instruments available to him were so crude that his calculations were bound to be inaccurate, and Pytheas was to get the circumference of Britain badly wrong.

His original narration was lost soon after its publication, and about all that we have of it are bits and pieces quoted by the contemporary historian Timaeus. It is quite possible that this Timaeus had talked in the harbours of Sicily to mariners who had actually sailed with Pytheas, and this may be why he, almost alone of the classical writers, does not dismiss the narrative as fiction. But since hints are all that we have to go by, we only get a vague picture of what Pytheas actually saw or heard on his great voyage of exploration. Yet we can tell at once that he *must* have had first-hand knowledge of Britain and the adjacent lands, for he could not otherwise have known of the Breton promontory of Brabant, of the islands in the open sea north of this promontory, of the general direction and shape of Britain, and of another island he calls Thule on the edge of the Arctic, a reference either to Iceland or Scandinavia. As for his observations about the people who inhabited these northern latitudes, they are of particular interest since they help to fill in the blank spaces of archaeological research – research which gives additional weight to the view that the navigator of Marseilles was the true discoverer of the British Isles, even though the Phoenicians were probably the first visitors.

His outward voyage, leaving Marseilles in the early spring in order to get as far north into the Atlantic as he could before the autumn gales, was full of interest. He evidently put in at Corbilo, a port in the estuary of the Loire, and saw British tin being unloaded. He was now able to meet the Gaulish and British skippers who ferried their flat-bottomed boats across the English Channel. Pytheas conversed freely with these Celtic sailors, no doubt through an interpreter, and found them friendly and far more civilized than the Greek savants allowed for. They told him how the tin was mined in Cornwall and how the whole of south-west England had prospered from the trade. Pytheas had, in short, discovered the source of the tin which supplied the Mediterranean market. He was told that the tin was cast into ingots, loaded on to pack-horses, and transferred to an island off the Cornish coast called Ictis.

It is assumed that the explorer navigated the island clockwise, probably sighting Ireland even if he did not land there, for he correctly positions that country to the west of Britain, while the geographer Strabo, who accepted the general verdict that Pytheas was an impostor, insists on placing Ireland to the *north* of the 'Pretanic Isles'. It would seem that the Massiliot landed frequently, for he had much to tell of the manners and customs of the Britons. He noted that the natives lived a primitive sort of life (archaeology makes this abundantly clear, as we shall see on our own expedition); fought from chariots in their tribal wars (as Caesar was to discover 300 years later); lived in houses constructed of logs; and stored their corn in underground silos.

> They are primitive in their habits and lacking in the guile of civilized men [he continues]. Their diet is plain and wholesome. The island is thickly populated and has an extremely chilly climate, as one would expect in a sub-arctic region. It has many kings and clan chieftains who live for the most part in a state of mutual peace.[3]

Everything that Pytheas reports here has been confirmed by the archaeologists, though there remain many puzzles which have kept scholars arguing and even quarrelling for centuries. Where, for instance, was Thule in relation to Britain? Six days sail to the north, says Pytheas, and one day's distance from the frozen Cronian Sea (unidentifiable). And round Thule itself there is neither sea nor air, but a mixture in which both are suspended in the atmosphere. Here there is perpetual night in the winter, perpetual day in the summer. Where are we to find this Thule? Is it Iceland or Scandinavia?

Here we must leave Pytheas *en route* eastwards across the North Sea to the Baltic, sailing as far as the Vistula in Poland

[3] This precis of Pytheas's actual narrative is found in Diodorus Siculus's *Bibliotheca Historica* (or, *History of the World*) V, 21.

according to some commentators, according to others stopping at the mouth of the Elbe. He certainly saw the lands where amber was cast up by the waves in spring and used by the natives (a German tribe called the Guttones) as firewood, or sold by them to their neighbours, the Teutoni. This report of the source of amber, one of the most valuable and sought-after products of the ancient world, was of special interest to the jewellers, apothecaries, and embalmers of the Mediterranean.

And so, having found the source of tin and amber in order to satisfy the merchants of Marseilles who underwrote his expedition, Pytheas returned to his native city and wrote his narrative *On the Ocean.* His voyage and his discoveries were among the greatest achievements of exploration and signal the beginning of the recorded history of our islands.

Something of what he saw and described in his account of his voyage is still visible to-day, as a glance at the maps of the *Ordnance Survey of Ancient Britain* will show. In the Northern Isles of Scotland alone, there are scores of Neolithic, Bronze, and Iron Age monuments still extant, suggesting that even regions which seem so inhospitable to-day were quite intensively populated in prehistoric times. Moreover, some of these monuments provide the archaeological evidence to support Pytheas's claim to have circumnavigated these unknown islands around the last quarter of the fourth century.

There is so much to see that it is difficult to know which region and which site to recommend. It is unlikely that many people will have the time or enthusiasm to make a special journey to, say, the little island of Mingulay in the Outer Hebrides to explore the Iron Age promontory fort of Sron an Duin, though this happens to be one of the most spectacular ruins in the British Isles. Yet it cannot be too emphatically stated that many prehistoric sites of exceptional significance to professional historians will be of no interest to the non-specialist, so that particular care has been taken in this survey to suggest places which are scenically rewarding as well as historically important.

HENGISTBURY HEAD (South Dorset): an Iron Age Trading Post

Guidebook: *Hengistbury Head*. Bournemouth Local Studies Publications. Bournemouth: Roman Press, 1979. (Available at the Red House Museum, Christchurch, Dorset)

Hengistbury Head was perhaps the most important harbour and trading post of Iron Age Britain and a likely place for Pytheas to have made his landfall. It is easy to reach by road from Christchurch, Dorset, where the Red House Museum contains the finds from the many 'digs' made on the Head. The

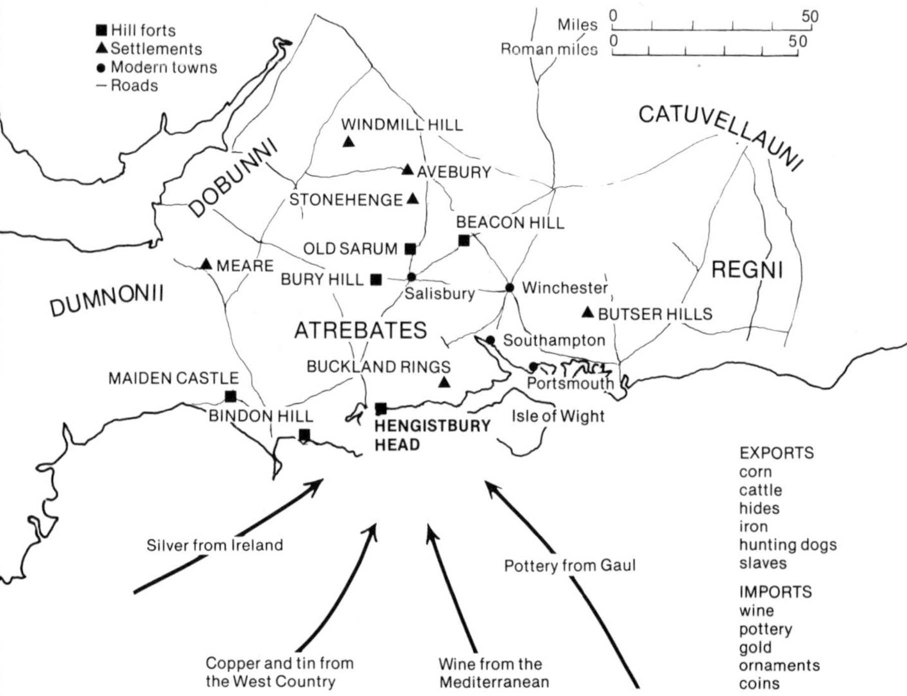

3 Map showing Hengistbury Head in relation to trading routes, and the exports and imports handled there.

Red House, in fact, is one of the best provincial museums in the country and should not be missed.

Hengistbury Head has become a very popular spot in summer for ramblers and dog-walkers, so the best time to avoid the crowds is early on a spring or autumn morning when the explorer will have the promontory and its wonderful views of the coast to himself. He should start his sightseeing at the Iron Age earthworks, or 'The Dykes', built to protect the settlement on the headland. Long before the Iron Age – as far back as 8000 BC – Neolithic hunters in pursuit of reindeers pitched their camps here, to be followed by new races of men right up to the end of the Roman occupation when the Head seems to have been abandoned. It represents a microcosm of early British history, reaching its pinnacle of prosperity as an international port in the time of Pytheas. Its long survival as a centre of trade and industry is evidence of the rise and fall of a succession of local kingdoms, making it one of the richest prehistoric sites in Britain. Unfortunately, archaeological excavations have meant the destruction of what few visible monuments have survived the centuries, so that it is no longer possible to see the eleven burial mounds which once added to the mystery of the place. But the headland still retains its special aura and even manages to remain largely unspoiled. It seems that as soon as it was abandoned by its human occupants, dozens of species of animals took up permanent or temporary residence, so that it is even possible, say the naturalists, to see the arrival and departure of birds like the Great White Heron, as rare now as the reindeer which passed this way 10,000 years ago.

From the coastguard station on the cliff top of Hengistbury Head the visitor can look out across Christchurch Bay to the Isle of Wight whose chalk pillars called the Needles mark the western end of the island. To the eye of the geologist this seascape is a land valley flooded during the Palaeolithic Age (12,000–8000 BC) when the Isle of Wight and the whole of the British Isles were joined to the continent. Hengistbury Head with its two adjacent rivers, the Stour and the Avon, was then a crossroads of prehistoric hunters who wandered back and forth across northern Europe following the herds of deer, boar, horse, and bison. They left behind many thousands of flint instruments, nearly 10,000 of which have been found by antiquaries within the last 80 years. Other finds unearthed during recent excavations include some 3000 Iron Age coins, ornaments, pottery, and imported objects like a Roman wine amphora. Many of these artefacts illustrating the importance of Hengistbury Head as a major British port before the Roman conquest are on view at the Red House Museum.

CARN BREA (Cornwall): an Iron Age Hillfort

Guidebook: H. O'Neil Hencken, *The Archaeology of Cornwall*. London: Methuen, 1932.

Almost every headland and commanding height in Iron Age Britain had its fortified settlement, and one of the best examples is the Cornish hillfort of Carn Brea, south-west of the town of Redruth, once the centre of the richest tin and copper mines in the world.

The site of the fort is best reached by a track from Carnkie and will be easily recognized from the ruins of the mediaeval castle on the eastern summit of the hill and the monument commemorating Sir Francis Bassett, sheriff and vice-admiral during the reign of Charles I. From the highest point of Carn Brea one can see Land's End to the west, the Cornish coast to the north, and the St Austell clay-pits to the east. On the southern slopes are the original defence walls, consisting of an outer and inner rampart divided by a ditch. Inside the thirty-six-acre enclosure of the fort there was a village of at least a hundred round huts. Only traces of these huts remain. Their inhabitants were probably tin-workers, for tin was the source of Cornwall's prosperity for a thousand years before the Roman conquest of Britain.

4 Prehistoric Britain, particularly the south and west, was notable for its hillforts, of which Maiden Castle in Dorset is the best preserved.

The first antiquarian to recognize the importance of Carn Brea was Dr William Borlase who surveyed and described the great hillfort in 1748. Unfortunately this clergyman became so carried away with the contemporary obsession with Druids that he mistook what was a village community of tin workers and farm labourers for the principal seat of Druidic worship in

Britain, nominating various rocks as monuments of that cult – here a sacred circle, there a stone idol, and somewhere else the Throne of Judgment.

Later excavations by nineteenth- and twentieth-century archaeologists have, of course, debunked Dr Borlase's Druids, but they have also left us with an even more disturbed terrain, so that it is now virtually impossible to visualise this site as the busy and important community it must have been from 1000 BC up to the fourth century AD when the settlement was abandoned.

Yet Carn Brea, said to be our oldest fortified settlement, can still provide a glimpse of an archetypal British village, not all that different from a mediaeval hamlet. Excavations indicate that the villagers lived in simple timber-framed shelters, tilled small plots of land, and kept flocks and herds on the hillsides. They were skilled enough to build dry-stone walls enclosing 36 acres of arable land. Within these defences, they erected 15 large circular huts, manufactured enough pots for their domestic needs, and specialized in the production of stone and flint tools. Carn Brea, as a prehistoric settlement, complements Hengistbury Head, the Bronze Age port and trading post.

Finds of several hundred leaf-shaped arrow-heads from the Neolithic age and a hoard of coins from later periods are displayed in the Museum at Truro, Cornwall.

JARLSHOF (Shetland): an Iron Age Farmstead

Guidebook: L. R. Laing, *Orkney and Shetland. An Archaeological Guide*. Newton Abbot: David and Charles, 1974.

For a long time the far north of Britain tended to be neglected by prehistorians despite the great number and excellent state of preservation of the ancient monuments. The reason for this neglect was the remoteness of the sites, many of them still difficult of access. Yet Scotland is probably richer in visible

5 The fortress-farmhouse of Jarlshof was the 'capital' of Stone Age immigrants who arrived in the Shetlands over 3000 years ago. The site they selected was occupied almost continuously until modern times.

Iron Age ruins than even southern England. The Northern Isles in particular have hundreds of splendid monuments, notably the circular towers called *brochs*, two hundred of which are still standing in Shetland and the Orkneys. The impression one gets from a tour of Iron Age Scotland is that the rural regions were possibly more intensively cultivated and more densely populated in the fourth century BC than they are to-day.

Jarlshof in Shetland is one of the most unusual Iron Age sites in the British Isles – one of the most important archaeological monuments in Europe, since it represents some 2000 years of almost continuous occupation from the Stone Age to modern times. Moreover, Jarlshof's appearance on the archaeological scene is sensational, for it emerged from nowhere in 1896 after a storm eroded the hillock on which stood the ruined mansion of the laird William Bruce. Overnight the archaeologists were presented with a prehistoric monument which had scarcely been disturbed since it was abandoned, making it relatively simple to reconstruct the life and times of our distant ancestors who left their homes and tools and even their personal possessions *in situ*. To-day the visitor can see for himself how a vanished race of men built their houses, defended them against their enemies, developed a social structure, and organized their economy. In fact, there is enough evidence at Jarlshof to fill in the enormous gaps left by the loss of Pytheas's account of Iron Age Britain.

We learn from the Jarlshof site that these original Shetlanders lived in houses built of stone around a central blockhouse, depending for their livelihood upon farming, stock-raising, and fishing. Their diet was rich and varied, thanks to the abundance of sea food. Their needs were few and simple. The housewife required a few pots and pans which the local potter supplied. Her husband and sons needed weapons and tools which were manufactured by itinerant smiths. Their ornaments they often made themselves.

So much was common to Iron Age settlements everywhere in northern Europe, but what is unusual in the case of Jarlshof is the advanced state of the culture in view of its remoteness from the farmsteads of the south. If Pytheas meant by 'Thule' the Shetland Islands and not, as some think, Iceland or Scandinavia, then Jarlshof really was on 'the edge of the world', its storm-bound rocks a hundred miles off the north coast of Scotland and nearly six hundred from that busy port of Iron Age England on Hengistbury Head. One wonders how the first immigrants managed to reach Shetland and what they must have thought when they first sighted the awesome Sumbergh

Head on the southernmost tip of Shetland Mainland. Either they already knew there was something good there or they were lucky, for they found tucked in behind the promontory a safe harbour, good arable and grazing land, an inexhaustible supply of fish, fresh-water springs, and abundant building material in the form of workable stones. Early man asked for little more. And so Jarlshof, with its broch, stone-built huts, and storehouses, served its occupants well, until the drifting sands covered it. Otherwise there might be fishermen and crofters living on this Iron Age site to-day.

[2]

THE PHOENICIANS IN BRITAIN

From the Brittany peninsula it is two days' sail to the land of the Hibernians and the island of Albion. The Carthaginian Himilco (whose own account I have consulted) visited these places which are rich in lead and tin.

Avienus, *Ora Maritima*

About 150 BC in the month of April, Himilco, the Carthaginian admiral of the fleet, assembled sixty ships at Gades on the Atlantic side of the Pillars in preparation for an expedition to a group of islands called the Cassiterides.[1] Ten of the fleet were triremes with a crew of four officers, six petty officers, and sixty marines. When the trireme was not under sail, it was propelled by three banks of oars, thirty men to each side of the ship. It could travel at eight knots and overtake any enemy or pirate on the sea.

The admiral was not expecting any real trouble with hostile ships or with pirates like those who lurked about in the Mediterranean backwaters. He was sailing an uncharted sea where neither Greeks, Etruscans, nor Romans dared to go. They didn't go because they were afraid of dangers they had invented themselves, including the usual 'monsters of the deep'. But Carthaginian ships, and their Phoenician forefathers before them, had been exploring this Ocean for the last 1000 years or more, though they naturally told their rivals nothing about what they had discovered and, in particular, what

[1] The authority for the voyage of Himilco is the fourth century AD Latin writer, Rufus Festus Avienus, whose *Ora Maritima* (*Sea Coasts*) contains a report reputedly written by the Carthaginian admiral himself.

countries supplied them with gold, ivory, tin and amber.

Like all the other expeditions they sponsored, the Carthaginian merchants had not put up the money to finance a scientific exploration. The admiral's orders were to find a sea-route between the Cassiterides and Gades in order to wrest the monopoly of the tin trade from the Greek colony of Massilia (today Marseilles). For 1000 years the tin vital to the armaments manufacturers had been transported overland across Gaul for trans-shipment to the East Mediterranean arsenals. This much the Carthaginians knew; but where the precious metal was actually mined – where these Cassiterides or Tin Islands actually were – was still a secret known only to a few captains. The little information available in the state archives referred to a country called the *Pretanic Isles* which was the land of the Brythons.

Himilco's brief as given him by the oligarchs in Carthage was straightforward. He was to assemble all the ships he needed, both warships and merchantmen, and sail northwards along the Iberian coast to the port of Corbile on the Loire where agents had made contact with a Gallic tribe called the Veneti. His fast triremes were to reconnoitre the route which those ship masters who had made a crossing of the Bay previously stated to be extremely hazardous, for as soon as a vessel rounded the Sacred Promontory and turned eastwards it was liable to be in continual danger from the fierce tides and south-westerly gales. The journey was not to be undertaken in winter in any case, so the best time to set out from Gades was early spring when the days grew progressively longer as one sailed northwards until, so it was said, there were places on the rim of the Ocean where there was no night at all.

Once the fleet had arrived at Corbilo, the second stage of the expedition was to hire an Oestrymnidean pilot to take the fleet northwards along the coast and round the most fearsome promontory in the western Ocean (Ouessant – now Ushant). Some sixty miles due north from this promontory lay the Islands which were the location of the mysterious Cassiterides.

The admiral was not enthusiastic about entrusting his ships to a barbarian pirate, but his captains assured him that sailing in these waters was entirely different from anything their shipmates had experienced in the Western Alantic or Indian Ocean. The winds were unpredictable both in strength and direction; the seas abounded in submerged rocks; and the ebb tide ran at twelve knots in narrow channels, though this was hard to believe. So many dangers made a pilot imperative. The skies were so often clouded over that neither the sun nor the star Kochab by which the helmsman steered at night was always visible. At such times only local sailors could navigate by instinct, like those birds which made long journeys across oceans.

Himilco's fleet arrived at the port of Corbilo on the River Loire at the end of August, four months after setting out from Gades. It was already late in the season, so the admiral decided to beach his ships and establish a temporary trading station at the mouth of the river. The Carthaginians had learnt from long experience how best to deal with primitive people: the procedure was to bring gifts which the wives of the chieftains particularly treasured – jewels, perfumes, and fine clothes. The women were also very partial to beautiful ornaments and glassware which backward people were not able to manufacture themselves. Once the gifts had been accepted and permission given to start trading, the merchants felt free to travel inland in search of those rare commodities found only in distant places.

In the meantime, the Carthaginians learnt what they could of the Cassiterides from the Gauls, who were not, however, disposed to give away information for nothing. It seemed that there were several different descriptions of their exact location, though it was evident that they were situated somewhere off the most westerly peninsula of the Pretanic Isles. Himilco's agents also discovered that the inhabitants of this tin-rich country lived in huts and spent most of their time hunting and fishing. They were not, however, savages, like the aborigines of the

Fortunate Islands[2] or the fearsome creatures Admiral Hanno had encountered on the slopes of the mountain called the Chariot of the Gods north of the Southern Horn,[3] and which he had called *gorillas*. The Britons, the Gauls said, were hospitable to visitors, provided they came as friends. And there were many visitors, for there was a continual traffic between Britain and those countries situated around the northern sea. Some of these foreigners had even crossed that sea in little round boats made of wooden laths covered with leather.

The more the Carthaginians heard about the abundance of the precious metal found in Britain, the more determined they were to visit the region, and they looked forward eagerly to the fair weather which was supposed to come with the arrival of spring. They established good relations with the local population by giving them help and advice, especially in the art of building, both in wood and stone. Most of the sailors had settled down with women of the country, choosing from preference those with long blond hair, blue eyes, and rosy cheeks. And so when the pilots said that the time for voyaging was propitious and the necessary sacrifices had been made, the fleet set sail with the good wishes of a friendly people.

The voyage from the mouth of the Loire to St Michael's Mount in Cornwall is one that thousands of ships large and small make to-day, and it is still a passage fraught with difficulties and dangers, especially for small boats under sail. The ominous words of the *Channel Pilot*, 'Ushant must not be sighted', sum up the character of this rock-bound coast. The prudent sailor, therefore, will stand well out to sea, especially

[2] To-day, the Canaries, the aborigines of which were the *Guanches*, an early Stone Age people wiped out during the Spanish occupation of the Islands in the fifteenth century.

[3] The mountain called by the Carthaginian explorers *Chariot of the Gods* was probably Mount Kakoulima in the West African Republic of Guinea. The *Southern Horn* would be Sherbro Sound, with Sherbro Island the place where the Carthaginians caught and killed three female 'gorillas' (probably chimpanzees) whose skins they brought back to hang as trophies in the Temple of Moloch in Carthage.

along the coast of Brittany with its vestiges of submerged mountains and legends of sunken cities. Himilco's captains were well aware of the hazards while working their ships past the succession of islets, and must have been relieved to see the land sink away to the south as they headed for the coast of Britain.

The Britons in their hill-castles on the headlands saw the Carthaginian fleet approaching when it was still sixty miles off and knew at once from the size and shape of the vessels that they were foreigners who had come from far away. The question was whether they had come to plunder or to trade, and it was agreed that no chances should be taken. The people left their huts on the sea shore and in the valleys and retired to their fortified encampments. Spies were left in hiding to report on the visitors and their movements.

The pilots who had brought the fleet safely across the Channel anchored the ships in the lee of an island they called Ictis lying less than a mile off the promontory of Belerium. It was to this island that the inhabitants brought the tin to be loaded aboard cargo vessels continually arriving from kingdoms all round the German Sea. Ictis had become the centre of the European tin and bronze trade, and the wealth that trade engendered had made the western Britons the most prosperous of the northern tribes. It had made them, too, the most experienced in commercial transactions, so that when the Carthaginians saw how well organized everything was in this part of the world, they decided to display their more valuable wares for the natives to come and inspect rather than the cheap, mass-produced goods which appealed to less sophisticated customers. Having done this, they retired to their ships and awaited the beginning of negotiations.

In due course, a delegation of Britons led by their chiefs came down to the foreshore and after examining the glassware, jewels, and ornaments, indicated that they were prepared to do business. The Carthaginians, dressed in long tunics and conical hats, crossed over to the mainland. Both parties regarded each other with great interest. On the one side stood the tall, fair-haired Britons; on the other, the small, black-bearded Asiatics. And when the latter advanced bowing ceremoniously and intoning lengthy greetings in the oriental fashion, the Britons were puzzled, wondering if these strangers were offering themselves as slaves in return for a safe refuge from enemies who had driven them from their homeland. But the Gauls explained that these oddly dressed men came from a country far to the south and were by no means as servile as they looked; on the contrary, they were fearless seamen and wealthy merchants who had come to barter for tin.

The Carthaginians spent the autumn and winter of that year anchored on the landward side of St Michael's Mount. There were conferences on the admiral's flagship, and the traders were invited to visit the hillforts overlooking the bay. The visitors found the natives most hospitable and technologically more advanced than the negroes of the West African coast, though the Britons had not devised a system of writing, without which no nation could call itself civilized – a deficiency the historian must regret, since it means that he has no way of knowing the nature, extent, and influence of the prehistoric maritime trade promoted first by the Phoenicians, then by the Carthaginians. Phoenician history and the Phoenician people are known to us almost exclusively through the animadversions of their bitterest enemies, Jews, Greeks, and Romans. The Romans, in particular, and for good reason, loathed their Semitic rivals to such an extent that they were incapable of making even a pretence of being objective about them. The typical Carthaginian was caricatured as an obese Asiatic, a pompous, vulgar, and over-dressed hypocrite with his air of moral rectitude which ill accorded with his practice of burning children alive. Small wonder, then, that for the Romans after centuries of war, Carthage had to be 'deleted' and the Phoenicians, eastern and western, exterminated as a separate nation. Even when their city, like their empire, had vanished, Plutarch was still berating them: 'They are a people of a bitter and surly nature, abject to their rulers, tyrannical towards their subjects, and without any humour or kindness.'[4]

Yet it was these Levantines who were the greatest seafarers of the ancient world, who travelled farther and discovered more than even the early Cretan sea-captains whose voyages are dimly recalled in the story of Odysseus's wanderings. The Phoenicians circumnavigated Africa, leaving by the Red Sea and returning by the Pillars of Hercules; the Carthaginians discovered the principal islands in the Western Atlantic, the Canaries and the Azores. But not a word of their achievements has come down to us in their own language, for ironically the people who are reputed to have invented the alphabet have left us nothing in the way of written records, all traces of which were destroyed in the great holocaust of 140 BC. When it comes to finding out the extent of Punic discoveries, we have to rely on hearsay picked up in the Mediterranean ports by the Greek geographers. It was this sort of vague information about northern Europe which eventually reached the academics and appears in the treatises of Eratosthenes, Strabo, and Ptolemy. It is hardly surprising, therefore, that the whereabouts of such quasi-mythical islands as the Cassiterides became more controversial than ever; and writing *fifty years after Caesar's invasion of Britain*, Strabo is still guessing as to their precise location. Indeed, his guessing has kept scholars arguing ever since.

However, Strabo did make one specific statement that seems to provide a vital clue: he states categorically that the Cassiterides were ten in number and lay close together in the open sea north of Spain. On the basis of this evidence, many commentators assumed that these islands could be none other than the Scillies, the *Silurae Insulae* of the Romans. But the Roman surveyors who were searching Britain for precious metals – gold, silver, copper, and tin – found very little evidence of tin in the Scillies which they used as places of banishment for

[4] *Plutarch's Lives*. Translated by Aubrey Stewart and George Long. London: Bohn's Popular Library, 1923. Vol. 2, p. 84.

state prisoners. So if the Scillies were not, and could not be, the Cassiterides, where in the sea north of Spain were they?

The answer is found in a book by the Sicilian historian, Diodorus Siculus, who compiled an encyclopaedia of world knowledge in twenty-four books some time in the first century BC. Like other pedants of his time, Diodorus lifted whole passages from other writers, invented fanciful stories based on legend, and included in his work information he must have obtained from travellers. This information, in fact, is probably the only useful or reliable material he has left us. An example is found in that section of his *History* in which he gives us an eye-witness account of how and where the tin trade was conducted by the Carthaginians; and it is this passage which provides the vital clue as to the location of the Cassiterides. He says:

> The miners of Belerion [i.e. Cornwall] produce the tin by carefully working over the ground where the ore is found. The ground is stony, but it contains tin-bearing seams from which the metal is first extracted, then smelted and purified. They then beat the product into a mould shaped like an astragal and carry it to a certain island lying off Britain called Ictis. At ebb tide the land between the mainland and this island is left dry, permitting them to transport loads of the tin across to the island in carts. . . . Here the merchants buy the tin from the natives and ship it over to Gaul whence it is carried overland down to the mouth of the Rhone.[5]

Diodorus's account, which is far too factual to ignore, must settle the question once and for all, for there is certainly no other island off the coast of Britain which answers so precisely to this description as St Michael's Mount off the southern coast of Cornwall. In fact, the little harbour at the base of the Mount is still occasionally used by small freighters and in Victorian

[5] *Diodori Bibliotheca Historica*, V, 22. Stuttgart: Teubner, 1964. Translated from the Greek by James Wellard.

times was a regular port of call for shallow-draft vessels loading cargoes of tin brought across from the mainland at low water.[6] *Ictis*, 'a certain island lying off the coast of Britain', can only be St Michael's Mount.

The tinners of the Bronze and Early Iron Age would have collected the ore in 'streams' which fanned out from the parent-lode and ran down the hillside. The metal itself was extracted by washing and panning exactly as gold miners working on their own and without machinery still do to-day in, for instance, Alaska. First, the prehistoric tin miners crushed the larger lumps of tinstone by smashing them with stone hammers on nearby rocks, which are still pock-marked with cup-like cavities resulting from the pounding. Then, the small lumps of ore were ground down between querns. And finally the detritus was washed in a wooden trough until the pure tin separated from the 'slime'. The metal itself was smelted in a furnace built of blocks of granite and fired with layers of charcoal, and then cast into saddle-shaped ingots suitable for loading on the backs of donkeys. These ingots are referred to by Diodorus as *astragals*, a Greek word which has several meanings, none of them really applicable to ingots of metal. But what was certainly intended was a description of the H-shaped form which was standard for metal ingots during the Bronze Age, particularly those ingots intended for export. One such H-shaped ingot weighing 158 lbs was dredged up from Falmouth Harbour in 1886.[7] It proves that tin was not only mined in Cornwall, but smelted and beaten there into ingots, exactly as Diodorus states.

Rocks pitted by stone hammers, furnaces crudely constructed from granite blocks, finds of horn picks and bronze

[6] 'The Mount offers a good port, daily frequented by vessels, where cargoes of tin are sometimes taken aboard after having been transported, as in olden times, at low tide across the isthmus. Colliers of 500 tons burden can now enter the harbour, which is in the landward or sheltered side of the Mount.' Sir Charles Lyell, *Principles of Geology*, Twelfth edition. London: Murray, 1875. Vol. 1, p. 262.

[7] See p. 37.

tools abandoned in the tin-streams are artefacts which enable us to understand how the prehistoric miners operated and to realize that their methods of working remained relatively unchanged right up to mediaeval times. Shaft-mining replaced 'streaming' in the fifteenth century and proved to be a much more expensive and hazardous undertaking than the prehistoric method. Indeed, the Victorian Cornish tin-miner's job was probably the hardest and most dangerous in the world, not excluding the coal-miner's. The tin-miner often had to climb down hundreds of feet by a ladder with the temperature rising 1° Fahrenheit for every 53.5 feet descended. In the deepest mines the temperature reached 110° Fahrenheit, and the miners worked naked to the waist in half-hour shifts, while their mates dashed buckets of water over them. They reckoned to lose at least 5 lbs a day from sweating, and they wore a flannel shirt and trousers in order to absorb the perspiration and keep them warm when they stopped work. They also wore wide-brimmed hats to serve as protective helmets. To each hat a lighted candle was affixed by means of a lump of clay. Thus garbed, the miner crept along his one-man gallery with head bowed until he reached the rock face which he began to hack, his only light a flickering candle. After eight hours crouched in his tunnel, he would wriggle back along the gallery to the main shaft, and slowly climb the ladders to the surface or 'grass', as the miners called it, and then walk in the darkness, his clothes still wringing with sweat, to his cottage two or three miles away. For this he would earn around a pound a week for as long as his lungs held out.

The tin-mining scene in the days when Phoenician galleys lay off the coast was, of course, entirely different, as we have seen from the description left us by Diodorus of Sicily, and his is the only written testimony we have. Strangely enough, the Roman writers never mention Cornwall or its tin even after centuries of occupation and exploitation of the island's metals. Archaeologists are always hoping to find some evidence of the Phoenicians' presence in the form of vestiges of their trading stations, examples of their coins, and, above all, inscriptions in the Punic language. But unfortunately the enterprising merchant-adventurers from Tyre, Sidon, and Carthage left almost nothing as a memorial of their presence even in those places which we know they did colonize – Malta, Sicily, and Spain. Certainly their more remote posts along the west coast of Africa and up the Atlantic coast of Europe have rewarded the diggers with only a handful of artefacts. As for the Cassiterides, it is very unlikely that sea-traders from the Mediterranean would set up permanent trading posts in places which they could only visit three or four months of the year. Anybody who knows what the winter gales are like around the Cornish coast will appreciate that the Channel is no salutary place for small boats from the end of October to the beginning of May. All through the winter months the western peninsula of Britain would have been cut off from the continent, and for long periods, perhaps for years at a time, the Tin Islands would have remained unvisited by ships from the Mediterranean. Yet if we could find just one Punic tomb in Cornwall, the controversy of the Phoenician connection would be solved.[8] So far none has been found, and without conclusive evidence of this kind, some historians will, with Herodotus, doubt whether the Cassiterides existed at all; others will class them with the lost lands of Britain – Avalon and Lyonesse and the vanished islands of Celtic mythology; and still others will continue to insist that Diodorus of Sicily must have obtained his information from a sea-captain who had actually loaded his ship with Cornish tin in the little harbour at the base of 'that certain island' which he calls Ictis and we know as St Michael's Mount.

[8] Readers who wish to explore further the British-Phoenician connection are referred to Lieutenant-Colonel Lawrence Austine Waddell's *Phoenician Origin of the Britons, Scots and Anglo-Saxons* (London: Luzac, 1931). Colonel Waddell's theory is that 'the daring Phoenician pioneer mariners were, as I found by indisputable inscriptional and other evidence, *not Semites as hitherto supposed, but Aryans in Race, Speech, and Script. They were, besides, disclosed to be lineal blood-ancestors of the Britons and Scots*' (p. vi). He devotes 450 pages to affirming this thesis.

ST MICHAEL'S MOUNT (Cornwall): a Phoenician Port?

Guidebook: *St Michael's Mount. A Guide*. Norwich: Jarrold, 1978.

The Mount is connected with the mainland by a causeway some forty yards in width formed by fragments of rock and pebbles compacted by two currents of the sea sweeping round the rock at the flooding of the tide. This causeway is covered at high water when the Mount becomes an islet, as Diodorus the Sicilian describes it. The circumference of the Mount is about one mile at the base, gradually diminishing to the summit, which is 250 feet above sea-level. The fortified monastery of the Benedictines, now a castle, clings to the summit and overlooks a small harbour once much used by coasters loaded with timber and coal when inward-bound, china clay, copper ore, and pilchards when outward-bound.

To-day the chief activity of the Mount is tourism, and the throng of sightseers wending their way back and forth from mainland Marazion, or Market Jew, makes it difficult to visualize the little harbour as the haven of the Phoenician 'round ships'. But an observant visitor can readily see how the great granite rock would always have afforded shelter to coastal shipping and how the Mount might have been one of the principal ports of western Britain throughout prehistory, used both by the Gauls who came in their fast sailing ships and the Irish who arrived in their coracles. For some reason not satisfactorily explained, the Romans never exploited the Cornish tin mines, so that the sea trade between this part of Britain and the Mediterranean declined until Ictis was abandoned altogether as a port, and St Michael's Mount disappears from the records until the Christian hermits took up residence in the Dark Ages.

In the fourteenth and fifteenth centuries Cornish trade picked up again and it was decided to construct a harbour, built on the ruins of a Roman jetty, according to the old antiquaries. By the eighteenth century the anchorage was busier than ever,

6 St Michael's Mount, to-day a tourist resort, was probably the port of the Phoenician fleet which visited Cornwall 2500 years ago to barter for tin. The island on which the abbey now stands was known to the Romans as Ictis.

and Sir John St Aubyn enlarged the harbour to accommodate 40 vessels. From then onwards until the beginning of the twentieth century, the Mount was a small international port, with foreign ships arriving to load cargoes of copper, tin, china clay, and herring. These goods were still being carted across the causeway at low tide, exactly as they had been in Phoenician times.

The Mount was known in the Cornish language as *Cara Cowz in Clouze*, or 'The Grey Rock in the Woods', a curious name which can be explained according to some commentators by the vestiges of a submerged forest extending for some miles around the base of the rock. The modern name, St Michael's Mount, is derived from its patron saint who appeared to a sixth-century Celtic hermit living on the rock. A priory of Benedictine monks founded here in the tenth century was actually a cell of the great abbey of Mont St Michel in Normandy of which the English monastery is a smaller version. Henry V, during his wars with France, seized the monastery as French property and gave it first to King's College, Cambridge and subsequently to the nunnery of Sion in Middlesex. After the Dissolution, the monastery was used principally as a castle, especially during the Civil War when, along with the rest of Cornwall, it supported the king but surrendered to Cromwell's army in 1646. After the Restoration, it became the property of the St Aubyn family, the present proprietors.

THE SCILLY ISLANDS: the Cassiterides?

Guidebook: *The Standard Guide to the Isles of Scilly*. R. L. Bowley.

Some historians have argued strongly for the claim of the Scilly Isles to be the Cassiterides. Others have pointed out that while a little tin has been found there, the amount was not enough to make it worth the Phoenicians' while to exploit it. A glance at the chart of the fifty islets and scores of rocks of these, the most western, outposts of Britain will show why. The dangers attendant on errors in navigation and seamanship are so formidable that many people still dread the three-hour crossing by ferry from Penzance to Hugh Town, the capital of the largest island, St Mary's. Although a sea journey to the Scillies might be dangerous even to-day, it does not follow that the Phoenicians would never have risked a landfall if a plentiful supply of tin had been available. For it is now accepted by prehistorians that primitive sailors were not discouraged from making long or difficult sea passages by reason of either natural or navigational hazards. Since it is obvious that Stone Age man did cross wide and stormy seas, this phenomenal feat is explained by talking of 'hugging the shore': that is, creeping from port to port in oared boats. But the megalithic monuments built by a race of men who can be traced from the Mediterranean to the Arctic Circle show that there was constant migration by sea as by land. These prehistoric sailors had neither clocks, compasses, charts, nor any of the navigational aids without which a navigator to-day would refuse to put to sea. Yet they found their way, by night as by day, as the Polynesians still do, by using all the signs provided by nature – sun, stars, winds, tides, currents and coastal skylines.

So the formidable dangers that the Scillies present would not have unduly alarmed the Punic sea-captains, particularly seamen like Himilco, who led the expedition to the Cassiterides, or Hanno, who sailed down the west coast of Africa perhaps to within seven degrees of the equator. In any case, men had been visiting these westernmost islands of Europe from time immemorial; and the proof is visible to this day. The Scilly Islands have at least sixty-one burial mounds or barrows surviving from prehistoric times: that is, three times as many as in the whole of Cornwall. Some of these tombs are on now deserted islands. The immense toil which must have been expended in constructing so many monuments with no aids other than deer-horn picks and stone tools proves first, the density of the population; secondly, a high degree of social organization; and thirdly, by implication, the prosperity of the islands. In prehistoric times, the time when the Phoenicians were monopolizing international trade, the Scillies had become rich; and the source of their wealth could not have been anything else but tin.

Evidence for a Phoenician presence might have been found in the late Bronze Age tombs, if a local chieftain, for instance, had

7 Tresco, Scilly, is thought by some historians to be one of the Cassiterides, or Tin Islands, mentioned by Herodotus. A prehistoric chambered tomb, one of 61 discovered in the Scillies, was found here. Cromwell's Castle, the tower in the photograph, is part of the island's 3000-year history.

taken with him to his grave some prized possession whose provenance was Tyre or Sidon. But unfortunately all the known barrows of the island have long been looted, demolished for their building stones, or used as hideouts by smugglers; and the few modern excavations undertaken have not yielded much in the way of artefacts, other than a few sherds. However, the curious will find some fifteen barrows on the largest of the islands, St Mary's, including one of the best preserved near the edge of a high cliff on Porth Hellick Down. He will also enjoy visiting the uninhabited island of Samson which has nine covered galleries to investigate. The best stands upon North Hill from which one can see many of the islands and, weather permitting, the mainland of England. In all, ten of the Scillonian group have prehistoric barrows, all awaiting scientific study and the possibility of finding some plausible explanation of the wealth and prosperity of a region seemingly cut off from the trade routes of the ancient world.

TRURO (Cornwall): the Museum

Guidebook: *The County Museum. A Guide.* The Royal Institution of Cornwall: Truro, 1980.

Once a busy commercial port, TRURO was, and to a lesser extent still is, the centre of the Cornish tin industry. A hundred years ago, it was the principal stannary town of Cornwall with four smelting houses.

The Stannary (or Tin Mining) Courts of Devon and Cornwall were founded about 900 AD during the reign of Athelstan, grandson of King Alfred. Even before the establishment of Stannary Courts, the Cornish tinners had their own parliament near Callington on the west bank of the Tamar. Here they convened every seven or eight years to legislate on matters concerning the industry. Such a local 'parliament' undoubtedly goes back to tribal times when the Phoenicians were trading with Cornwall. In 1307 this parliament evolved into the Stannary Courts which dealt with questions of 'coinage' (the stamping of a seal on metal to guarantee its quality); 'tin-bounding' (the designation of areas where the miners were legally entitled to work); 'black' and 'white' tin (casserite and pure tin); and so on. The last Cornish parliament was convened in Truro in 1752; it and the independent Stannary Courts were abolished by Act of Parliament in 1896. Many Cornishmen feel that their ancient stannary rights should be returned to them.

8 Two of the artefacts now in the Truro Museum, an ingot of tin weighing 158 lbs, and the statuette of a bronze bull, were believed by the old antiquaries to be of Phoenician provenance. The ingot is certainly pre-Roman, the bull probably Egyptian.

To-day Truro is a holiday and tourist centre, and makes a most pleasant headquarters for students interested in prehistoric Cornwall, notably the tin industry and its relation to the Phoenicians. The only clues that we have to work with will be found in the Museum of the Royal Institution of Cornwall in Truro. It was established in 1818, and contains almost everything of archaeological and historical importance found in the county, notably the only three artefacts which have the remotest claim to being 'Phoenician'. The first of them is a unique ingot of tin dredged up at the mouth of the river Fal in 1812.

The block weighs 158 lbs and, most important, its peculiar H-shape is identical with that of the copper ingot found at Enkomi in Cyprus, known to date from the late Bronze Age (1200–1100 BC) and to have been especially cast for export. In other words, both the British and the Cypriot ingots were shaped for loading on the side of a pack animal, or storing in the hold of a ship. This peculiar form was referred to by the Sicilian writer Diodorus as 'astragalus-shaped', though it is evident that the Greek text here is corrupt, since ἀστράγἄλος, which can signify such different objects as 'one of the vertebrae', 'ball of the ankle-joint', 'a knuckle-bone as used in dice games', 'an architectural moulding', 'an ear-ring' and 'milk-vetch', is meaningless in this context. Nevertheless, the Truro ingot must date from a period when tin was cast in a form especially designed for shipment during the Bronze and early Iron Age. If submarine archaeology had been possible in 1812, perhaps divers might even have found the wreckage of the vessel which was loaded with the astragal-shaped ingots when it foundered in Falmouth Bay.

The second 'Phoenician' artefact in the Truro Museum has been equally controversial ever since it was found in the vicarage garden of St Just in Penwith. It is a little statuette of a bronze bull discovered in 1832 when workmen were demolishing 'an old building' to make way for a new school. The local antiquaries were certain that this little artefact was Phoenician, but Dr H. R. Hall, keeper of the Egyptian and

Assyrian Antiquities in the British Museum, pronounced it to be Egyptian from the Roman period. But the mystery remains. How did the little bull find its way down to St Just in Penwith, nearly the westernmost village of the British Isles?

The same questions could be asked of the third 'Phoenician' exhibit, the Numidian coin of the second century BC, said to have been unearthed at Carn Brea, the great prehistoric hill-castle near Land's End (pages 14–16). This coin has a bearded head on one side and a galloping horse on the reverse, and is usually attributed to the Numidian king Micipsa who reigned over a Carthaginian colony from BC 148–118. The galloping horse is presumably symbolic of the famous African cavalry which fought first for Carthage and then for Rome. It is tempting to speculate that it reached Cornwall in the purse of a Punic merchant, but although eighteenth-century antiquarians would be allowed to make such assumptions, to-day's strictly 'scientific' standards would not permit them.

With so little positive evidence to go on, historians tend to leave the controversy of the Cassiterides, or Ictis, and the Phoenician presence in Britain well alone; but for those who have no academic status to put at risk, there remain some entertaining theories to examine and some interesting sites to explore, especially in the fortified Bronze and Iron Age settlements built on or near the Cornish coast. Examples are Carn Euny midway between Land's End and Penzance, and Castle-an-Dinas, 2¼ miles ESE of St Columb Major. Many of these circular hillforts had rich deposits of tin close by, which suggests that they could have had commercial connections with the Phoenicians and Carthaginians. Finds of imported pottery and foreign coins are evidence of international trade between these Cornish settlements and the Mediterranean lands long before the Roman conquest of Britain, but there have never been enough trained archaeologists to explore in depth the many Bronze and Iron Age sites in western Britain. It is unlikely, therefore, that we shall ever know much more than the ancient historians tell us.

[3]
BRITANNIA FELIX

The Britons submit themselves cheerfully to military service, taxation, and other burdens imposed by our government, so long as they are fairly treated. Of wrongs they are impatient. Even when broken in to obedience, they still refuse to serve as slaves.

Tacitus, *Agricola*

'I get up at eight o'clock in the morning,' writes Decimus Magnus Ausonius,

> awakened by the sun streaming through the windows and our house swallow twittering in her nest. I shout for my valet to bring me my slippers and dressing gown. While I am having a quick wash, he prepares my private chapel where I conduct morning prayers. (I have to admit that some of the servants find my daily report to the Almighty somewhat verbose. But then they only speak pidgin-Latin and don't really understand what I am saying.) The service over, I get ready to go out visiting, but first have a conference with the cook, Sosias, about lunch. "Lunch to-day is for six, Sosias, including myself the host." Conference over, I call in my secretary, a fellow whose shorthand is so good he can keep up with me as fast as I dictate. In fact, the man seems to know what I am going to say before I say it. Does this mean that I am a little obvious? . . . Never mind. . . . 'Take a letter to Parmenus. . . .'[1]

[1] These details are taken from *The Poems of Ausonius*. English translation by Hugh J. Evelyn White. London: Heinemann, 1919, pp. 13–31.

9 The mosaic of a North African villa, from the Bardo Museum, Tunis, illustrates the architecture of a rich landowner's farmhouse of the type built all over southern Britain during the Roman occupation.

The time is around AD 340; the place, a villa in south-western France; the writer, a country gentleman with an estate of over 1000 acres consisting of vineyards, cultivated fields, pastures, and woods – beside a river which takes him by boat to the nearest towns and home again. His estate, he writes, is near enough to Bordeaux for convenience and yet far enough for him to escape the crowds. He is, in short, a rich, prosperous ('fruits in store to last me two whole years'), and happy man who spends his time farming, hunting, fishing, and writing *opuscula*, or 'poetic trifles' (some of them hundreds of lines long) to amuse his friends.

There was really no difference between the world of Decimus Magnus Ausonius and that of a contemporary Romano-British landowner, except, perhaps, that Ausonius was a raconteur of such banality that he must have sent his listeners fast asleep. It is this very prolixity that is so precious to the historian to-day, for he speaks to us as a real human being across sixteen centuries, saying, in effect, 'Here is a day in the life of a provincial Roman gentleman. This is what it was like.'

Unfortunately similar letters and diaries by British contemporaries of Ausonius have not survived, though there must certainly have been many an aristocrat for whom literature was as much part of life as hunting and fishing. Ausonius actually refers to one such Briton, a poet called Silvius Bonus who evidently criticized the Romanized Gaul's effusions. In a typically heavy-handed epigram Ausonius strikes back: 'Silvius hic Bonus est, sed Brito est Silvius idem: simplicior res est, credite, Brito malus.'[2]

So we know that there was at least one well-known British poet writing around AD 340, and there were undoubtedly other authors apart from the Christian exegetes, one or two of whom we shall meet later. But we have nothing comparable with the *belles lettres* produced in almost every other province of the Empire. The Africans, for instance, have left us a whole library of fascinating books, including the best novel of the classical era, Apuleius's *Golden Ass*, and the best theological treatise, Augustine's *City of God*. Egypt, Syria, Spain, Sicily, Gaul, all produced historians, essayists, poets, and diarists of distinction, men who strove to uphold the old intellectual standards in a world which was moving relentlessly into the Dark Ages and, at the same time, told us what *everyday life*, as distinct from historical events, was like. It is all the more regrettable that not a single British writer does the same thing for Roman Britain.

But we do have abundant material evidence of Roman Britain, despite the absence of literary testimony. We have the evidence of an enormous number and variety of Roman remains strewn across the length and breadth of the land. In

[2] *Ausonius, op.cit.* p. 216. Translation:
'Here we have Silvius Good. But this particular Silvius is a Briton. Believe me, if he is a Briton, he can't be good.'

particular, the archaeologists have unearthed some splendid specimens of the kind of country mansion where rich landowners like Ausonius lived, the large, comfortable Roman villa, or farmhouse, found all over the Empire. It was these villas with their extensive and well-run estates which helped to change barbarian Britain into *Britannia Felix*. Some were as commodious and luxurious as the best of our 'stately homes' to-day, centrally heated, carpeted, as it were, with mosaics, and beautified with wall paintings. Such villas imply prosperity and security for their owners, and justify the description of Roman Britain as 'Happy', a land of milk and honey, with pastures almost too deep for the cattle, and hillsides covered with flocks of sheep whose udders were bursting with milk and whose backs were weighed down with wool. Scores of cities and towns and country estates belonging to this *Britannia Felix* still dot our landscapes, and the problem is where to go to see the best examples of this extraordinarily productive period in our history. For productive it was, as shown by the evidence of thousands of ruined monuments – towns, villas, castles, temples, fortresses, marching camps, roads, even lighthouses and signal stations. These monuments constitute only the visible relics of an intensive occupation which lasted over four centuries. Underneath our cities or below the farms and fields lie many more sites whose outlines are plainly revealed by aerial photography. The archaeologists tell us that scores of these sites are being lost every year, and it has become a familiar spectacle to see teams of devoted professional and amateur diggers desperately trying to find out what they can before the bulldozers demolish another irreplaceable landmark of our heritage.

Yet despite the wealth of ruins, it is not easy to tell from them what Britain was like in, say, AD 306 when Constantine was proclaimed emperor in York. We need to find something more evocative than fragments of walls, broken pavements, truncated columns, odds and ends of sherds, and so forth. For how otherwise can we explain why the Romans, who imposed their language on this island, abolished the tribal societies, persuaded the farmers and herdsmen to leave their hill fortresses and move down into the valleys – practically swept away the old Celtic culture of the Britain of Pytheas and the Phoenicians – had no sooner left these islands than they and all their works seem to have vanished, as it were, overnight? Latin became as incomprehensible to the ordinary natives of these islands as the language spoken here during the neolithic age. The highly sophisticated complex of roads, cities, and forts, with the temples, forums, baths, arenas, and aqueducts which the conquerors had built, were suddenly unwanted and unused, as though the people who had built them had never been here at all.

And yet the Roman presence in Britain is more pervasive than we realize. It permeates the very landscape. For what the invaders did was to change Britain from a country covered by dense forests into something resembling the still unspoilt regions of, say, Sussex. These conquerors even affected the climate, at least ameliorated it, by clearing vast tracts of forests, cultivating the plains, and draining acres of water-logged bogs and fens formerly given over to wolves, bears, the aurochs or wild ox, and wild boar. All accounts of the early travellers emphasize this dankness, caused by the continual rains and chilly air even in the summer, the forests attracting and condensing the moisture, the crops unable to ripen, the streams obstructed by fallen timber, and the rivers lost in reedy marshes.

The proof of the profound change in the manners and customs of the Britons is seen by contrasting their living standards before and after the Roman conquest. Before the conquest, they were, in the opinion of observers from the Mediterranean, a 'surly and savage race', constantly at war with each other; the men spent most of their time preparing for battle, attempting to insult and provoke their foe, and after the conflict rushing about in their chariots holding aloft the severed heads of the enemy. The victorious soldier, says Caius Julius

Solinus, drinks his enemy's blood and smears his face with gore.[3] As Caesar had found in his day, the barbarians of Gaul, Germany, and Britain were all great practitioners of 'frightfulness' and knew little of, and cared less for, the arts of peace.

But after the conquest and once these barbarians were civilized, their leaders could pass for 'Romans' anywhere in the vast Empire. The serfs of the tribal nobility for their part, and even the slaves of the Romano-British landowners, had a higher standard of living than before, for certainly their housing and diet were improved. They seem to have been a rather merry crowd, for we have a discourse by one of them in a contemporary drama called *The Pot of Gold*, written and performed somewhere in southern Gaul around AD 400.[4] In this play, the slave Pantomalus points out that his master is really a very unreasonable and disagreeable man, because if something is stolen, he goes around cursing as if theft were a crime! Still, the poor man has a dreary existence compared with us (says Pantomalus), for every day we have a marriage or a birthday. We have continual games, parties, and outings. In fact, we don't want to be emancipated at all. No thanks! For who but a slave could have so much fun at so little expense?[5]

But Pantomalus is a stage character, and no doubt life was very different for the real slaves; but judging from the evidence of the kitchen-midden found during excavations of the Roman villas dotted about the English countryside, there was at least an abundance of food, and it seems probable that everyone, master and man, mistress and maid servant, ate reasonably well. The citizens of small towns had a choice in the market of wild boar and venison as well as beef, mutton, and pork. Sea food, including shellfish, was abundant and cheap. There was

[3] Caius Julius Solinus, *The Excellent and Pleasant Works*. Translated . . . 1587, by Arthur Golding. A facsimile reproduction. Gainesville, 1955. Cap. xxxiiii.

[4] From *Querolus* (*Le Grognen*). Traduit par Léon Herrmann. Bruxelles: Librairie M. Lamertin, 1937.

[5] *op. cit.*, pp. 29–31.

not, of course, as great a choice in fruit and vegetables as there is to-day, but there was always plenty of whatever produce was in season. Almost every Roman villa, really the headquarters of an estate, had bathing facilities superior to those of most working-class homes to-day; the buildings were centrally heated; rooms were embellished with tessellated floors and painted walls; and the family could look out of their windows on to open courtyards enhanced with flowers and fountains.

All these obvious improvements in living standards have led some historians to argue that Britain under the Romans and, for that matter, all the occupied countries of western Europe, were better governed and better organized than they ever had been before and, some would argue, have been ever since. It is an interesting theory. Its advocates point out that the old hatred of the Romans which had inspired tribal leaders like Boadicea and Caratacus during the first years of occupation had been replaced by the pride of being a Roman citizen. Tribalism was almost dead. Britons were no longer barbarians. They belonged to One World, not a small clan; and their loyalty was to a king-emperor, not a local strong man. Belonging to this world community, they were able to travel from York in the north of Britain to Germa on the edge of the Sahara Desert, from Exeter in the west to Palmyra in the east, without the formalities of passports, customs regulations, foreign currencies, or diverse languages. Above all, they inherited a marvellously rich culture based on the art and philosophy of Greece and the laws and technology of Rome. It is true that this culture was largely confined to the educated classes, but this is the nature of culture in any age, to-day as in fourth-century Europe. The peasantry were semi or wholly illiterate, but the impression is that they were neither ignorant nor uncouth. There were theatres all over the Roman world which, like the theatres of Elizabethan England, attracted ordinary folk as well as the *literati*, though the amphitheatres which staged shows of revolting cruelty were much more popular with the masses. Certainly the English country gentry of the Roman period were more literate than the fox-hunting squires of the reign of George III, and as readers of good books, prided themselves on their libraries. The mosaic floors of their villas show how familiar they were with the classical authors. In fact, the British monk Fastidius chides his fellow-countrymen for having time to read Virgil, Sallust, Terence, and Cicero, while neglecting the writings of the Fathers.

Perhaps the greatest achievement of this civilizing process was the new status of women who were no longer regarded as chattels, but as the equals of men in intelligence, education, and ability. The names and writings of many of these women of the Empire are still remembered – Hedibia of Armorica, Paula, Bassula, Palladia, Theresia. Their lives and works prove that they were completely emancipated, to such an extent, indeed, that some of them rejected all thoughts of marriage and family life in order to dedicate themselves to medicine or literature or travel. Nor were such feminists regarded as suffragettes and condemned for unwomanly behaviour. On the contrary, they were greatly respected and encouraged in their chosen careers. It is just possible that one of these remarkable women was British, for we have a reference to a traveller who 'came from the farthest shore of the Ocean'. The Ocean was the Atlantic, and Britain was always described as being on its outermost limit. At all events, this lady undertook a journey of exploration through the Middle East comparable with the fascinating voyages of the Victorian women-explorers, and her description of Palestine in the fourth-century has luckily survived.[6] It is one of the best travel books of the time, thanks to her curiosity and delight in all that she saw, plus a certain raciness in the actual account of her experiences.

But as far as we know, Britain did not produce any women writers comparable with the Grecian Sappho or the Roman Sulpicia. Neither was it renowned for its male poets, historians,

[6] *The Pilgrimage of S. Silvia*. Translated by J. H. Bernard. London: Palestine Pilgrims' Text Society, 1891.

and philosophers. The exception was the monk Pelagius, perhaps the most interesting heretic in Christian history, whose writings prove how vigorous was the philosophical and speculative thought in a province once so remote from the gr[illegible] centres of learning in Athens, Rome, and Alexandria. P[illegible]gius's Celtic name is said to have been Morgan, thou[illegible] evidently he was not Welsh but Irish. St Jerome refers to him[illegible] *Scotus* which meant in the fourth century a native of Ireland. The sarcastic Father obviously disliked Pelagius, for he scoffs at the Irishman's paunch, which he described as being 'stuffed with Scottish porridge' (*Scotorum pultibus praegravatus*). But whatever Pelagius's appearance and diet, he was certainly no country bumpkin. If anything, he was more of a Roman than the Dalmatian St Jerome. Latin was his language; scholarship his vocation; theology his avocation. His manners were such that he was as much at home in the great houses of southern Gaul, Italy, and Africa as he was in the villas of his native Britain. An international language and excellent communications enabled him to travel all over the Empire, first to Rome, where he proclaimed his controversial doctrine of the Free Will, next to Sicily, thence to North Africa, and eventually to Palestine, accompanied by another Irish monk called Coelestius. Pelagius met in the course of his journeys all the great theologians of the age – Rufinus in Rome, St Augustine in Carthage, Grosius in Jerusalem, St Jerome in Bethlehem. We see, then, how a Briton, in common with scholars, teachers, businessmen, and commercial travellers from every point of the compass, was able to travel without let or hindrance from end to end of the known world. It was a Golden Age for intellectuals. And the intellectual brilliance of a scholar like Pelagius, born and brought up in a country which had only recently been described as inhabited by cannibals, proves how profoundly the Graeco-Roman culture had penetrated into the farthest corners of the barbarian kingdoms of northern Europe. And yet this Irishman, educated, it is thought, at the Welsh monastic school at Bangor, is quintessentially British (i.e., Celtic) in his innate dislike of authority, whether civil or religious. This was all very well in a Celtic country, but where the Roman Church was concerned, any questioning of official doctrine was tantamount to heresy. Pelagius's temerity in challenging Rome finally led to his downfall.

What, then, were these 'British' ideas that he and Coelestius were promulgating in the very capital of the Church? First, that the doctrine of Original Sin was unacceptable, since we could not be held responsible for Adam's conduct. Secondly, every baby born is as innocent as Adam before the Fall, whence baptism of infants is meaningless. Thirdly, it is possible to continue in a state of innocence, to live without sin, provided a man *willed* it. Fourthly, if a man had Faith, he could gain eternal life by his own efforts – without help from above. Fifthly, prayer for the conversion of others is futile, since it cannot help them unless they themselves freely will their own salvation. And finally, God is only a spectator, and not an actor in the human drama.

The extraordinary phenomenon of a British monk propounding ideas which were to affect the thinking of the entire civilized world – the phenomenon of a man born in the remotest province of the Empire yet able to defend himself in Greek at the Council of Jerusalem in AD 415 (his Spanish opponent Orosius could only speak in Latin), is taken by some to justify and, indeed, glorify the Roman occupation of Britain. But critics of that occupation, while admitting that a few privileged natives of these islands were well educated in the classical tradition, paint a very different picture of the actual conditions during the period. They point to the brutal attack on a small and weak nation in which a brave and independent people were first crushed by a ruthless military machine, then reduced to slavery or serfdom, and finally conscripted and taxed to an unendurable degree. Admittedly the peasants of Britain never openly revolted as they did in Gaul and Spain, so presumably they were not so cruelly abused. Even so, these critics argue, while the Romans introduced civilization into Britain in the material sense, they did so at the expense of the liberty and dignity of the conquered. Their Empire was built on the ruins of small nations. It was bound to collapse, and when it did, Roman Britain fell an easy prey to barbarians who swept away almost every vestige of the Latin culture in a few decades.

Some historians have compared the Roman administration of Britain with the British administration of India, to the extent that the people of both occupied countries benefited from the interdiction by their masters of barbarous customs – Druidism with its human sacrifices in Roman Britain, *suttee* with its immolation of widows in British India. And where humane and wise governors, supported by efficient district commissioners, did their best to dispense impartial justice, the ordinary people were protected from, not subjected to, tyranny. Tribal kings were often persuaded to abandon their traditional warrior role and to embrace the politics of peace and prosperity. A classic example from Roman Britain was the chieftain of the Belgic tribe who accepted senatorial rank (*rex et legatus Augusti in Britannia*) and called himself King Tiberius Claudius Cogidubnus, in return for submission to, and co-operation with, his conquerors. His reward was a palace designed for him by Roman architects and built by Roman masons, a Versailles, estimated to have cost in current terms about two million pounds. Its splendid ruins can still be seen near Chichester in the suburb of Fishbourne, symbolizing the wealth and prosperity that the Roman conquest and the romanization of the barbarian king had brought to the region.

But there can be no doubt that the Romans decided to conquer Britain not to elevate the natives but to exploit the land. In the beginning they were disappointed, for Julius Caesar had discovered during his expeditions of 55 and 54 that the country was so primitive that its people did not even know how to grow corn and, on mature reflection, was hardly worth the effort of conquest. The Emperor Claudius, however, went ahead with the plan of occupying this outpost of western Europe probably for reasons of self-glorification; and once it was occupied, the victors set about getting what commercial gains they could from the enterprise. They had hoped, above all, for gold, having noted that every Celtic chief had so enriched himself with this precious metal that even his horses had gold breastplates. What they did not know was that most of this gold came from Ireland. So while they undoubtedly hoped to find gold mines in Britain, they actually found only one, at Dolaucothi in Wales. As a compensation, however, Britain was rich in lead which was mined principally for its silver content; and very soon lead mines were being worked in Somerset, Flintshire, Yorkshire, Northumberland, and Derbyshire.

The Romans were experienced miners and throughout the duration of their Empire were burrowing away all over the known world, excavating millions of tons of metal and stone, thanks to the efforts of slaves, convicts, and some primitive machinery. Their methods of mining had not greatly changed or improved since neolithic times. They had no particular incentive to improve conditions of work, since mines had always been regarded as prison camps. Condemnation *ad metalla* ('to the mines') was no less a terrible punishment than condemnation *ad bestia* ('to the arena'). And while we have no direct evidence as to the treatment of British miners, we know from literary sources, and in particular the writings of Christian witnesses, that Roman mines, whether of metal or stone, were veritable concentration camps. In the worst mines – those of Numidia and Palestine, for instance – the workers were always fettered and chained together even while working. Some were deliberately hamstrung to eliminate even the dream of escaping. Others were blinded in one eye to brand them as felons. Miners, both men and women, worked in shifts throughout the day and night, guarded by barbarian soldiers who did not speak their language and were therefore not susceptible to bribery.

There is little now left at the Dolaucothi gold mine to enable us to reconstruct the scene as it was when the Romans were there, though the underground galleries driven deep into the hillside and the three aqueducts, one of them seven miles long, are proof that many hundreds, perhaps thousands, of men were employed in the operations.

We do not have a single account by a contemporary British writer of what everyday life was like for *any* member of the community, let alone the miners, but we do have some hints embedded in a religious tract written by an ecclesiastic referred to as 'Fastidius, a Briton'. Nothing else is known of this man except what he tells us in his voluminous correspondence, and, reading between the lines, that is quite a lot. He tells us, for instance, that he had set out on a long and perilous journey to the East (we do not know where he started from), but got only as far as Sicily where 'I found a lady who dissuaded me from going any farther. . . . Finding her devotion, her faith, and her learning well-known to the laity as well as the priests, I handed myself over to her entirely.'[7]

Having settled down comfortably with this good woman, Fastidius proceeds to lecture his correspondents back in Britain on the wickedness of the world. Nearly all sinful behaviour, he says, originates from 1) lust and 2) avarice. We can fairly assume that he had reached this conclusion from what he had seen in his own country where he had grown up and actually married, for he refers to a daughter he wishes his father to take care of now that he has settled down with this pious Sicilian lady. In the meantime, he has worked out a method for resisting the temptations of the flesh: it is to avoid women altogether, for, he says, 'they are like the sellers of spurious commodities who dread the scrutiny of a strict examination'; and he clinches his argument by stating that since a true Christian ought to hate the world, which is going to end one day in any case, there is no point in continuing to populate it. Procreation, he declares, can be left to Jews, heathens, and

[7] *The Works of Fastidius*. Edited and translated by R. S. T. Haslehurst. London: The Society of SS Peter and Paul Limited, 1927. p. 15.

heretics. Christians will steadfastly avoid sexual intercourse, for 'having something in common with pigs and dogs is nothing to be particularly proud of'.[8]

One is bound to get the impression from these letters that Fastidius had witnessed such a lamentable state of affairs in Britain that he despaired of his countrymen, and obviously something had happened there to account for his dislike not only of holy matrimony, but of wives in particular and women in general. And after he has finished condemning concupiscence, he directs his wrath against the capitalist system itself and so can lay claim to being the first British socialist. One can hear his voice very clearly across almost fifteen centuries. His denunciations could be used word for word in a Party Political Broadcast to-day, except that they are too elegantly expressed. His thesis is that wealth is the result of sin, a contention he proves by the following argument: 'I assert, and no wise man can dispute it, that Wealth is obtained chiefly by clever lying, skilful theft, fraudulent disloyalty, violent robbery, or barefaced adulteration.'[9]

Fastidius was not condemning those Christian landowners who lived in palatial villas, like the one at Lullingstone with its Christian chapel, but *pagans* who were not only prosperous, but were enjoying life as well. One of them we have already met, his contemporary across the Channel, the very luke-warm Christian but very pagan-minded Ausonius, who far from decrying the pleasures of the flesh, extols the joys thereof. For instance, he had acquired as booty on a military expedition a blonde German girl whom he brought back to his villa in the south of France. One can imagine the scene, the apprehension of this captive torn away from her family and home and assigned to an elderly gent who could not even converse with her. But this sad picture very quickly changes, and what we see next is this portrait of the prisoner:

[8] *op. cit.*, p. 283.

[9] *ibid.*, p. 8.

> Bissula, born and bred beyond the chilly Rhine not far from the source of the Danube; Bissula, who was a prize of war, a captive I have freed, now queens it over me! Lacking a mother, wanting a nurse, and not having a mistress's control, she rules her master. She has not been so changed by becoming a Roman, but remains a blue-eyed, golden-haired German girl – my pet, my love, my joy. . . .[10]

Bissula, the German slave-girl whose story has such a happy ending, has a British counterpart. Her name is Regina and she had evidently been taken a prisoner by the Romans during an uprising of her tribe and then sold to a Syrian tradesman. We know of her from the inscription on her tomb where she appears seated, holding the symbols of status as a housewife – the jewel-box and the work-basket. The dedicatory inscription underneath reads:

> DM. REGINA. LIBERTA. ET. CONIUGE.
> BARATES. PALMYRENUS. NATIONE.
> CATVALLAVNA. AN. XXX

> This monument is dedicated to Regina, whom Barates, a citizen of Palmyra, liberated and made his wife. She belonged to the Catuvellaunian tribe. She died aged 30.

And underneath the formal Latin, Barates had inscribed in the Palmyrene language the words 'Regina, alas!'

These two mementoes of Roman provincial life give us a glimpse of what Britain was like when a Caesar ruled it. An elderly Celtic landowner's infatuation with his German mistress, a Syrian merchant's grief for his British wife – the two men both Roman citizens, the two women both liberated slaves – tell us more, perhaps, than the ruins of cities.

As for ruins, the Romans were in Britain for four centuries,

[10] *Ausonius*. With an English translation by Hugh G. Evelyn White. London: Heinemann, 1919. Vol. 1, p. 221.

and since they were certainly one of the most industrious people of all time, it is hardly surprising that our land is littered with relics of their occupation. The enthusiast can even follow them to the west coast of Wales and the far north of Scotland. Wherever they went, if only for a short stay, they left behind some tangible souvenir of their presence – a marching camp, an inscription, a memorial to a dead comrade. Consequently nobody could conceivably visit all the Roman remains in Britain in one lifetime, and he would have to be something of a fanatic to want to do so. For the majority of the Roman monuments which have survived here are architecturally very ordinary in comparison with the magnificent ruins found all round the Mediterranean littoral; and many of the remains which sound quite interesting on paper prove, *in situ*, to be little more than unidentifiable rubble.

In view of this, I have suggested three sites which, while not as spectacular as the legionary camp at Caerleon, South Wales, none the less illustrate some lesser known aspects of Romano-British life.

COLCHESTER (Essex): the First Romano-British City

Guidebook: *Colonia Claudia Victricensis. The Story of Roman Colchester.* Issued by the Museum and Municipal Committee, Colchester.

Camulodunum, the capital of King Cymbeline (Cunobelinus) and the most important town of Celtic Britain, became the Colonia Claudia Victricensis of the Romans, the Colecestra of the Saxons, and the Colchester we know to-day. It is a town with at least 2000 years of continuous history; and the best place to begin a study of the Roman period is the Norman castle built on the original foundations of the great temple dedicated in AD 49 to the Emperor Claudius, who was called 'divine' even while he was still alive. Claudius had arrived in Britain just in time to witness the siege and capture of Cymbeline's capital, an event which marked the beginnings of the conquest and Romanization of Britain. A model of the temple exhibited near the Museum entrance is especially worth examining, since it was this building which the desperate Romans defended for two days against the army of Queen Boadicea. The temple was captured, looted, and then destroyed. Only the substructure survived. Those interested in seeing the original Roman stonework can visit the vaults by request.

The two most important souvenirs of the Colchester of Claudius were found in the rubble and ashes of the Roman city – the tombstones of a Thracian cavalryman called Longinus and the statue of a Roman infantryman, Marcus Favonius Facilis, centurion of the 12th Legion. Both are beautifully displayed in the Museum, and both are worth detailed study, for they represent the very essence of the Roman army in its heyday. The cavalryman Longinus came from a barbarian tribe famed for horsemanship; the centurion Facilis from Rome itself. He is dressed in active service uniform, or battle dress. A cuirass protects his chest and belly, greaves his knees and ankles. Over his armour he wears a loose cloak and round his waist a two-tiered leather kilt. His weapons consist of a short sword, or *gladius*, and a dagger (*pugio*). He carries neither shield nor spear, but a vine-staff, symbol of his authority and an instrument for punishing misdemeanours in the ranks. Because of what it tells us about an officer of the Roman army, the tombstone of Facilis is one of the most interesting artefacts ever found in Britain.

As for the other relics of Roman Colchester, there is a fair amount to see outside the Museum, though nothing spectacular as ancient monuments go. But sections of the original Roman walls have survived, despite the destruction of the civil wars and the deliberate demolitions of modern planners. It is possible to make a circuit of the original Colonia Claudia Victricensis, stopping at the Balkerne Gate which in Roman times was the entrance for the London-Colchester road. The

10 The Roman centurion, Marcus Favonius Facilis, was buried at Colchester, or, as he would have called it, Colonia Claudia Victricensis. He is a personification of the legions which conquered Britain.

size of the gate even in its present ruined form proves how important was this first military and political capital of the newly conquered province.

It did not remain so for long, however, for it was soon to be superseded by London as the administrative and commercial centre of the province, especially after it was totally destroyed in the rebellion of AD 60 led by the queen of the Iceni tribe, Boadicea.[11] The Greek historian Dion Cassius (AD 155–235) gives a description of this amazon who was to become the idealization of Britannia herself:

> Tall in stature, hard-visaged, and with fierce eyes, a rough voice, and bright yellow hair tumbling down to her waist, she wore a great golden collar over a many-coloured tunic which was bound closely under her bosom. Over her tunic she wore a thick mantle fastened with a gold clasp. And in her right hand she bore a lance.[12]

This was the woman who led an army of 100,000 Britons determined to avenge the scourging of their queen and the ravishing of her daughters. The first objective of this barbarian force was the undefended settlement of Colonia Claudia, where a handful of Roman soldiers, most of them veterans who had been settled in the town, made a last stand in the great temple. The fearful end of the first Roman city to be established in Britain is described by Tacitus, son-in-law of the island's greatest governor, Agricola. Tacitus was writing only a few years after Boadicea's sack of the city:

> The commanding general Suetonius being far away, the citizens of Colonia Claudia appealed for help to Catus

[11] The queen's Celtic name was Boudicca, meaning 'The Victorious'. But Boadicea has passed into folk-lore, and it is now too late and too pedantic to change it.

[12] Dion Cassius, *Roman History*. Translated by Ernest Cary, Ph.D. London: Heinemann, 1907 (The Loeb Classical Library). Vol. 7, p. 63.

Decianus the Procurator, who sent them a force of barely two hundred ill-armed recruits, with a sprinkling of regular soldiers. For defence, they relied on the temple; but as they were unaware that their plans were known by the spies of Boadicea, they dug no trenches and erected no palisades. They also omitted to send the old men and women away. Now they were surrounded by a multitude of barbarians. The temple was stormed after a siege of two days. . . . No less than 70,000 citizens and allies were slain in Colonia (Colchester), Verulamium (St Albans), and London.* For the barbarians would have nothing but killing, whether by sword, cross, gibbet, or fire as though hurrying to avenge themselves beforehand for the retribution which was to follow.[13]

Colonia Claudia Victricensis was rebuilt, and this time it was defended with walls in the manner of all Roman towns. It is presumed the settlement had six gates, but only one, the Balkerne, gives some idea of Roman Colchester. This gate, which resembles more a triumphal arch than the usual fortified town-entrance, has provision for two-way vehicular traffic with pedestrian walks on either side. Such a monumental arch is in keeping with a city which was named after the conqueror of Britain and which claimed to be the birthplace of Constantine the Great.

After the departure of the Romans, the 'Colony of Claudius, the Victor' became the headquarters of various warring bands, Saxons, Danes, Normans, and eventually the English kings right up to the reign of Charles I. The population was from time to time 'put to the sword' by the victorious armies, but Colchester always survived as a busy market town and river port.

[13] *The Annals of Tacitus*. Translated by George Gilbert Ramsay. London: Murray, 1909. Book IV, Chapters 31–2. pp. 209–10.

* An obvious exaggeration, typical of Roman historians.

PORTCHESTER (Hampshire): a Roman Naval Station

Guidebook. *Portchester Castle*, Hampshire. London: Ministry of Works. Leaflet Guides, 1943.

Portus Adurni, to-day Portchester Castle at the head of Portsmouth Harbour close to the village of Portchester, belongs to a somewhat neglected area of Roman-British history: the role played by the imperial navy in the conquest, exploration, and defence of the British Isles. Once the legions had suppressed or pacified the tribes and the province became prosperous, the chief danger to security came from the North Sea pirates, making the protection of the seas, particularly around the eastern and southern coasts, of paramount importance. For this purpose, a chain of naval stations was built and a special fleet, the *classis britannica*, formed. The warships operated out of harbours protected by forts, the best preserved of them being Portus Adurni whose walls still stand twenty feet high and ten feet thick, enclosing an area large enough to have accommodated two Roman legions and, fifteen centuries later, 8000 French prisoners captured during the Napoleonic wars.

Portus Adurni is thought to have been built around AD 290 by a Belgian sea-captain called M. Aurelius Mausaeus Carausius who declared himself emperor of Britain and actually reigned from 286–93 as a 'brother' of Diocletian and Maximilian. His 'realm' included northern Gaul where he established a sort of imperial court at Boulogne. Like most usurpers, he was soon assassinated, but not before he had built the great naval station at Portus Adurni. His fleet consisted of large galleys for the marine commandos and light craft for reconnaissance. The galleys were propelled by oars, the skiffs by sails. The crews were not slaves, but, like the Roman soldiers, were freemen entitled to full citizenship at the end of their service. They were commanded by a captain responsible for navigation, and his crew included a boatswain, a sailmaster, a surgeon, a carpenter, and various petty officers. The flagship

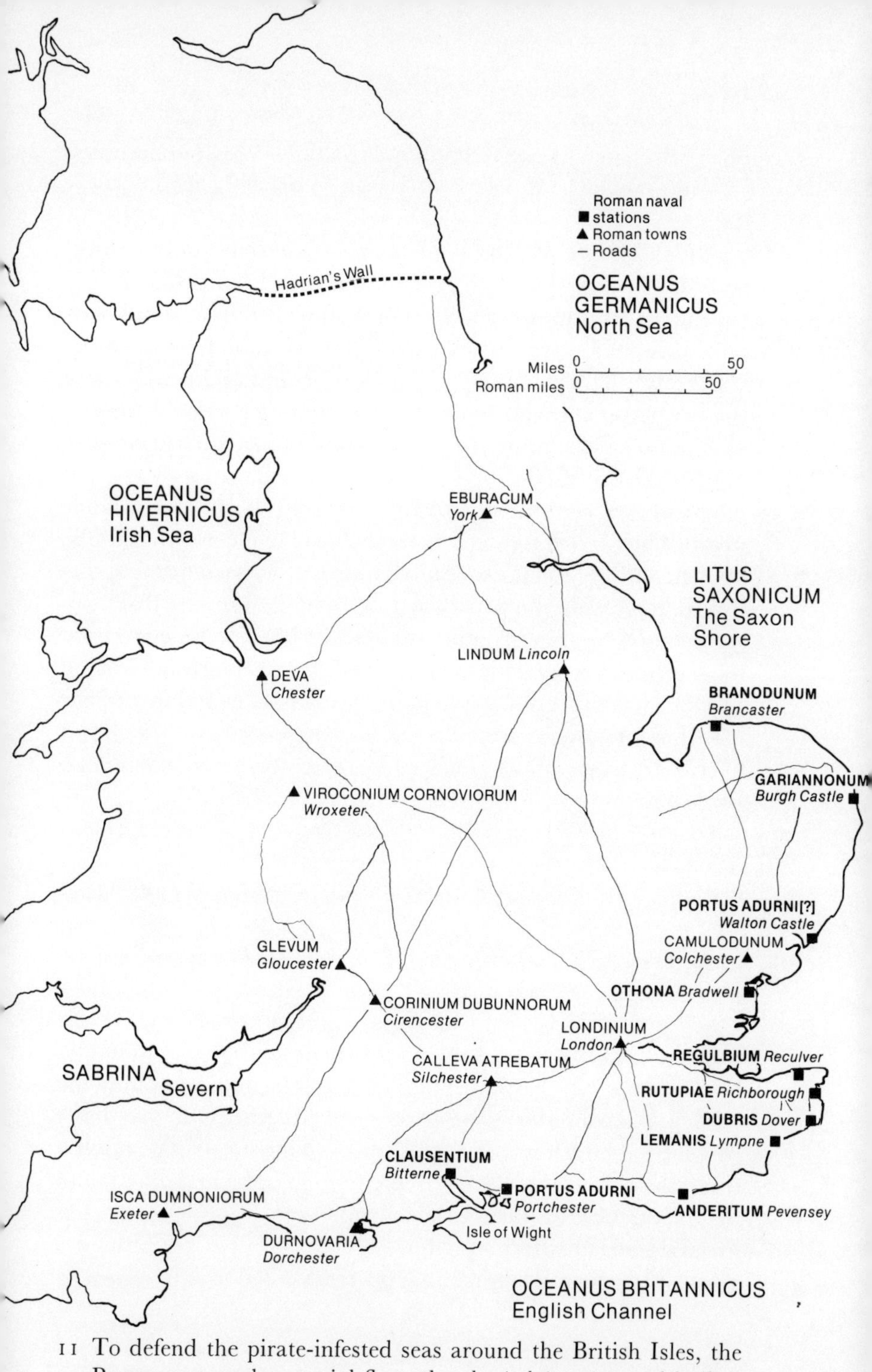

11 To defend the pirate-infested seas around the British Isles, the Romans created a special fleet, the *classis britannica*, and built a chain of naval stations along the eastern, southern, and western coasts. The largest of these fortified harbours was Portus Adurni, to-day Portchester Castle.

of the fleet would also have regular ship's clerks, including a stenographer and a priest in charge of dressing ship on holy days.

About AD 370, Portus Adurni was replaced by another naval base farther to the west at Glausentum, to-day Bitterne, a suburb of Southampton. It is not known why a station as powerful as Portus Adurni should have fallen into disuse. Certainly the Normans realized its potential and converted it into a royal castle whose massive keep still dominates the upper reaches of Portsmouth harbour. From the twelfth century onwards it was used primarily as a royal residence and hunting lodge, and during the nineteenth century as a prisoner-of-war camp. The French soldiers' graffiti can still be seen on the walls, and the tales of what they suffered as they were herded by the thousands inside the prison are capped by the story that they were so hungry they ate a British officer's horse tethered outside the Norman keep, hooves, tail, and all. In contrast a shipload of French girls captured on the high seas and taken to Portchester Castle as prisoners were allowed to attend parties and balls all over Hampshire. Before long, everyone of them had married an Englishman.

DOLAUCOTHI (Carmarthenshire, Wales): a Roman Gold Mine

Guide Book: J. B. D. Jones and P. R. Lewis, *The Roman Gold Mines at Dolaucothi*. Carmarthen, 1971.

Dolaucothi is the site of the only British gold mine worked by the Romans, who exploited it to the limit, for gold was one of the principal economic arguments used to justify the expense involved in the conquest of Britain. The site of the mining operations does not immediately reveal the extent of the Roman activities, because the tunnels, open-cast workings, underground galleries, and aqueducts are not easy to find without a guide. Moreover, Dolaucothi has been worked over by prospec-

12 The Romans burrowed deep into the Welsh hillside at Dolaucothi mining for gold. Little remains to be seen of their extensive workings except for entrances to the galleries, traces of aqueducts, and water tanks. The photograph shows one of the entrances to the Romans' mine at Dolaucothi.

tors and mining syndicates ever since the Romans abandoned the site.

To reach Dolaucothi, now owned by the National Trust, the visitor should make the historic town of Llandovery his headquarters and proceed from there to the hamlet of Pumpsaint where signs will direct him to the Roman mine. A fine day and, if possible, a knowledgeable guide will make all the difference to his enjoyment of the expedition.

It will be immediately obvious to the visitor that such a large-scale enterprise before the introduction of earth-moving machinery necessitated the recruitment of thousands of slaves, 1) to drive the tunnels into the hillside, one of them traced to a depth of 145 feet; 2) to construct the three aqueducts, one of which brought water from seven miles away; and 3) to hew out of the rock the great terminal reservoir which collected 5000 gallons of water a day for washing out the gold from the crushed ore.

The evidence from other mines elsewhere in the Roman world helps us to understand how the shafts were driven deep into the Welsh hillside, how hammers and wedges were used to break up the rock, and how, working by the light of little terracotta lamps, the workers at the rock face hacked out the gold-bearing ore. The chief problem, as in nearly all mines, was flooding. Where drainage was essential, slaves were set to work with buckets to bale non-stop into tanks from which pumps lifted the water to the surface. Fragments of such a pump have been found at Dolaucothi and can now be seen in the National Museum of Wales at Cardiff. Archaeologists have also found remnants of the mill stones by which the ore brought from the mine was crushed before being washed to extract the gold. We know, too, from a contemporary description of a mine in Sicily that the capstan which rotated the mill stone was often worked by women: 'standing two or three together at one spoke of the capstan, filthy and almost naked women work a long shift, and to every one of them assigned to this task death is better than life'.[14]

We have no way of knowing whether British women captured during the continual fighting against the Welsh tribes were used in this manner, but they were probably present at Dolaucothi in the role of camp-followers, for the mines were guarded by troops from Caerleon, headquarters of the 2nd Augusta Legion.

[14] Diodorus of Sicily, *The Historical Library*. Translated by C. H. Oldfather. London: Heinemann, 1933 (The Loeb Classical Library). Vol. ii, p. 79.

The vestiges of a military camp at Dolaucothi emphasize the importance the Romans attached to the gold mine despite the wildness of the terrain. There was also a bath-house nearby, probably for the use of the guards, for it seems most unlikely that the slaves working the mines were indulged with the luxury of a bath. There is no mining camp, something of a mystery, for the workers had to be housed, even if under the crudest conditions. One can only assume that their huts, which they no doubt erected themselves, have long since tumbled down, for this unique example of Roman enterprise in Britain was not properly discovered and surveyed until the 1960s. Yet the Dolaucothi mine illustrates many of the most impressive achievements of Roman technology and deserves further study. As it is, a visit to this picturesque region of Wales helps at least to suggest how industrialized Roman Britain had become as early as AD 200.

[4]

GODS AND GHOSTS: THE RELIGIONS OF ROMAN BRITAIN

The various modes of worship which prevailed in the Roman world were all considered by the people as equally true; by the philosopher as equally false; and by the magistrate as equally useful.

Edward Gibbon,
Decline and Fall of the Roman Empire,
Ch. 2

On the morning of December 25, AD 302, Gnaius Arrius Claudianus, a wealthy London merchant, set out to attend divine service at the Temple of Mithras by the River Thames.[1] To-day was the nativity of the Redeemer who had come to save mankind by the shedding of the sacrificial blood: *Et nos servasti eternali sanguine fuso*, as the inscription across the vault of the temple proclaimed. The London Mithraeum had only recently been built at considerable expense, all the furnishings, statues, sacred dishes, et cetera having been imported from Italy. The marble altar at the end of the nave was especially fine and most beautifully illuminated, as befitted a shrine for the celebration of communion which was to be held this morning with the traditional breaking of bread and drinking of wine.

Arrius took his appointed place on one of the benches which flanked the nave, bent his head in prayer, and tried to put aside the mundane thoughts which usually occupied the mind of a busy merchant, for this was a very special day, the birthday of Mithras himself, and it was only fitting for a man who has just been initiated into the Order of the Raven to renew his vows to

[1] Originally in the Walbrook. Now at Temple Court, 11, Victoria Street.

13 The shrines of the Mother goddesses (the Matres) were found all over Celtic Europe. This example of Romano-British sculpture shows the deities, some with their offerings of fruit, and one with a baby.

the Lord of Light. Raising his head to see who was present, he noted the air of expectation among the congregation, for divine service this morning was to be conducted by a Syrian Father who had been admitted to the seventh degree only last year after attaining international reputation as a Courier of the Sun. Arrius as a Briton was particularly interested to hear what this eminent Syrian had to say on the subject of the Nazarenes who were being accused of stealing on behalf of their Jewish god the doctrines as well as the rituals of Mithras.

The wall lamps were now extinguished and only the candles behind the altar were left burning as the Syrian Father in his red Phyrgian cap and crimson tunic entered and raised his right hand in benediction; and as he approached the altar, the

14 Bronze statuettes of Venus were popular as ornaments throughout the Roman provinces; but the existence of this example from Verulamium (St Albans) does not mean that the cult of the goddess was observed in Britain.

curtains were suddenly parted to reveal the god himself in his flying cloak and about to plunge his knife into the bull. More candles were lit, the bell tinkled, a great shout went through the temple, signifying that the Lord was among them. Now the hidden choir began to intone the Creed: 'I believe in Mithras, Lord of the Wide Pastures, he who cleft the rock to release the life-giving waters. We are his sheep and he is our shepherd. . . .'

The recitation of the Creed was followed by the singing of the nativity hymn telling of the adoration of the shepherds on the night that the god was born. The temple was now in darkness except for the shining figure of Mithras turning his head to listen to the message of the celestial raven. The worshippers fell silent. The Syrian Father began to speak.

> Be watchful, for the Day of Reckoning is nigh. On that day Mithras himself will descend from his throne to summon all men from their tombs. They will stand before the Judgment Seat; the just will be separated from the unjust. The just will be rewarded with eternal life; the unjust will be destroyed by fire. . . .

Arrius was disappointed. He had heard all this many times before and he expected something more original from a man of such distinction. The Father must have stopped off in Rome on his way to London, so what had he heard about the emperor's current religious policy? Was it true that he was looking with favour upon the Christians who were now asserting that their god was the only true King of Kings and Lord of Lords, while openly canvassing for the support of peasants, women, and slaves? If so, these bigots would next demand that the temples of Mithras be closed and the brotherhood proscribed. This would surely be tantamount to undermining the political and social system itself, for it was the army and the city that maintained that system, and the religion of the soldier and merchant was Mithraism. Why wasn't the Syrian warning them of these dangers and exhorting them to remember that they were the élite, chosen to defend the God of Truth?

Gn. Arrius Claudianus was right in calling the followers of Mithras the élite. Membership in the order was almost exclusively limited to the military and commercial classes and was hardly known outside the legionary camps and large towns. Such a stern religion, with its emphasis on morality and self-denial, was singularly unattractive to animists like the Britons who had their own pantheon of local gods, personifications of thunder, lightning, trees, and rivers.

It seems likely that these gods were venerated because they provided the excuse for seasonal get-togethers in the tradition of country fairs. We can guess this much by noting the locale of the sacred places – sylvan groves, lakes hidden in woods, fountains of pure water, medicinal springs, and so forth. The folk who foregathered in such pleasant spots had come not just on a pilgrimage, but on holiday, in the same spirit as Chaucer's company set out on their Canterbury pilgrimage. And once the rituals had been observed, the pilgrims looked forward to some rustic merry-making. The high point of such festivals was the feast when the burnt offerings were consumed. In this respect the Druid ceremonies must have been especially popular, for Pliny states that after the mistletoe had been gathered by a priest in a white robe, *two* white bulls were sacrificed for the feast which followed. For the congregation of peasants, artisans, and serfs who had not tasted meat perhaps in months, the sound of the incantations, the sight of the sparks from the pyre flying skywards, and, above all, the odour of roasting flesh were as inspiring as holy communion to the devotees of Mithras.

The more the gods and goddesses, the more the festivals. On the evidence of inscriptions alone, we know of nearly one hundred gods who were worshipped in Britain during the Roman occupation. Many of these deities were not autochthonous, but were imported by administrators, soldiers, and merchants from all over the Empire, thus adding variety and perhaps confusion, to the religious scene. But we can guess that rural Britons preferred their own homely divinities to the official deities of their conquerors or the importations from the Orient; and since it was the Roman policy not to interfere with other peoples' idols, the British gods continued to flourish, although many of them were the crudest of fetishes and must have literally astounded an intelligent Roman who saw their devotees abasing themselves before such totems. An example is the so-called Wheel God, Taranis, whose effigy was dug up in Corstopitum (Corbridge in Northumberland), a Roman supply depot behind Hadrian's Wall. The archaeologists themselves dubbed this simulacrum 'Harry Lauder', obviously on account of his kilts, knobbly stick, and slight air of inebriation. Was Taranis really taken seriously by his devotees? And did wheelwrights actually pray to him for special concessions? We can ask the same question about the contemporaries of Taranis, deities we only know from their names, names which are bizarre enough in themselves – Antenociticus, Cocidius, Huitris, Behalennia, Nodens, Thincsus, and Wharfe.

One of these Celtic divinities is of special interest on account of the splendid temple erected to him at a time when the pagan gods were being ousted by Christianity. His shrine was found at Lydney Park near Chepstow in Gloucestershire. The site is on a private estate, and cannot be visited without permission. But the ruins of the temple, the pilgrims' rest house, and the extensive baths which yielded an enormous and varied number of artefacts have been so destroyed or disturbed by generations of archaeologists, both amateur and professional, that there is little left to see. The visitor is advised to go dressed as for a walk over a grouse moor, so overgrown is the ancient site. Nevertheless it was here at Lydney Park that the last of the old nature gods held court and may even for a little while have rivalled in Britain the powerful new official religion of the Empire, Christianity. The god was Nodens, and he is a somewhat mysterious member of the Celtic pantheon, though real enough to his worshippers who left their votive offerings, inscriptions, and coins (hundreds of these) at his shrine. We think he was a god of hunting, or possibly fishing, since a mosaic in his temple, now destroyed, had a frieze of sea-monsters and fish, suggesting some connection between the god and the sea. There were also a great many representations of dogs found in and around the temple, a fact which the layman would assume confirms Nodens's role as a hunter. The experts tell us, however, that the dog was associated with healing, and numbers of them were kept in temples dedicated to Asclepius for the express purpose of healing infections by licking the patient's wounds.

The Temple of Nodens was finally destroyed by foreign raiders, probably by the Scotti from Ireland some time in the fifth century. The destruction of such holy places, like the destruction of the villas which dotted a prosperous and peaceful countryside, came rapidly after the withdrawal of the last of the legions. Nodens now passed out of men's memories, along with Taranis, Antenociticus, Cocidius, Huitris, and even the most powerful of the cults, Druidism, which Caesar had considered his most dangerous adversary. It was the Druids who inspired and, in practice, governed the people. They were omniscient, for they had a monopoly of learning; they were rich, being exempt from taxation and military service; and they were political dictators, since they monopolized both the civil and criminal jurisidiction. They certainly did not at all resemble the Druids who turn up today at Stonehenge on the occasion of the summer solstice, each robed in white, crowned with an oak wreath, and dignified with a pastoral crook. We have a description of what they really looked like by the historian Tacitus who based his report on information supplied by officers who had fought at the Battle of the Menai Straits in AD 61, the year the Romans intended to invade the Isle of Anglesey by fording the straits at low water. Tacitus tells us that when the legionnaires of the 14th and 20th started to cross, they were momentarily halted by the spectacle on the other shore: the ranks of the British formations parted and out came a band of women howling like banshees, their hair streaming in the wind and their torches blazing as the Druids, standing well to the rear,

15 Stonehenge has long been associated with Druidic rituals. Even to-day, votaries of the ancient British priesthood come to this prehistoric monument on the summer solstice to see the sun rise.

stoked the fires on which they were roasting their human sacrifices.[2] Tacitus's description reminds us more of the Incas of Peru than of the natives of these islands, but his account is circumstantially confirmed by the 1946 excavations at Llyn Cerrig Bach on Anglesey which unearthed the principal shrine of the British Druids.

Druidism depended upon primitive magic for its credibility – divination by sneezing, the croaking of ravens, and the chirping of wrens. Mithraism, in contrast, was an essentially ethical movement, dedicated to the virtues of civil duty, physical courage, and the control of the passions. It was a male-oriented cult which appealed particularly to professional soldiers and so,

[2] *Tacitus*, op. cit. Book XIV, chapters 29, 30.

by implication, excluded women from its communion. In common with all secret fraternal organizations, it was characterized by the sort of mummery which impresses the otherwise practical citizen – underground sanctuaries, flickering lights, mystic symbols, and painful initiation ceremonies. It had seven orders, beginning with the Order of the Raven and rising through the degrees of Bridegroom, Soldier, Lion, Persian, Courier of the Sun, to the highest rank of Father. Divine service was accompanied by symbolic rites involving sacrifices, drinking of blood, and oblation of consecrated bread. In the ceremony of the *taurobolium* celebrating the slaying of the bull by the god, the penitent was placed in a pit covered over with planks having spaces between them. A bull was led on to this platform and with due incantations was slaughtered by the priests so that the blood streaming from its throat flooded through the cracks on to the votary below. In order that not a drop of this precious, life-enhancing fluid should be wasted, the baptized crawled about under the platform so as to get himself thoroughly drenched in blood. The object was to achieve a spiritual cleansing, with a promise of eternal life to come.

So impressive to serious-minded men were its rituals and beliefs that Mithraism might even have become the official religion of the West, had not the Christian Church triumphed in the struggle for political power and so established a base from which to destroy not only the doctrines but the temples of its rivals. On the other hand, the seeds of its own decay may have been dormant in the rigid and uncompromising dogma which denied spiritual fellowship to those very people who had most need of it – women and peasants and slaves. It was inevitable that a gentle Jesus was to displace a stern Mithras as the saviour of mankind, even though the Christ of the Jews was as alien to the Britons as the Mithras of the Persians. The Celtic serf, harassed by enemies, human and animal, could hardly be expected to comprehend the Christian exhortation to turn the other cheek, and was probably more confused by the new religion than a highly intelligent Roman like the Emperor

Hadrian, who could not distinguish between the Egyptian Serapis and the Jewish Jesus, since both seemed to stress the art of healing, Serapis by means of medicine, Jesus by means of miracles.

In the meantime, Christianity had come to Roman Britain, as it came to every other province of the Empire, through the medium of soldiers (perhaps Jewish), commercial travellers, and the occasional slave in the retinue of a state administrator. But there were not many such evangelists, and converts must have been few. Even after Constantine's decision in 312 to adopt Christ as the official deity of the army and the Empire, the pagan gods were still popular, and Britain did not become a Christian country until long after the Romans had gone. Certainly not a single building dating from the occupation has been positively identified as a church, whereas Africa Proconsularis, for instance, had scores, some of them on the borders of the Sahara Desert.[3]

Christian antiquities of Romano-British origin are rare. The principal examples are the wall paintings from a villa at Lullingstone, Kent; a mosaic floor with a portrait of Christ from Hinton St Mary in Dorset; and traces of Christian worship in the form of the chi-rho symbol displayed on the mosaics of the reception rooms of Roman villas at Frampton, Gloucestershire and Chedworth in the Cotswolds. From Water Newton in Cambridgeshire comes a hoard of silverware (now in the British Museum) with many of the vessels bearing Christian motifs and inscriptions. There is a possibility that this plate was deliberately removed from a Christian shrine and carefully hidden during one of the periods of persecution, although some historians argue that the imperial edicts never affected British Christians to the extent that they did their African and Asian brethren, and they cite as evidence the lack of martyrs and the absence of catacombs found all over the Mediterranean world.

[3] See James Wellard, *The Great Sahara*. London: Hutchinson, 1964. Chapter 5, pp. 95–109.

The most we can assume is that Christians and pagans lived peacefully side by side in Roman Britain, with the new faith making converts among officials and landowners as soon as Christianity became the state religion and paganism was officially proscribed. But the beginnings of the faith in these islands are still shrouded in mystery, due principally to the absence of contemporary records. Admittedly the African theologian Tertullian, writing about AD 200, states that 'parts of the island [Britain] not yet controlled by the Romans have surrendered to Christ'. But Tertullian could have known next to nothing about this distant land, and when the ecclesiastical historians came to write the story of the origins of the Church, they knew little more and had to fall back on legend to explain how the gospel was brought here. The honour of being our first evangelist was eventually bestowed on Joseph of Arimathaea. Joseph, they said, arrived from Jerusalem with 150 disciples early in the first century AD to found an oratory at Glastonbury in Somerset, bringing with him the sacred thorn tree and two silver cruets, one containing the blood, the other the sweat, of the crucified Christ. This legend which seems to argue for a British 'first' over all the Christian nations of the West was fiercely contested both by the French, who point to the prior arrival in Provence of SS. Mary and Martha, and by the Spanish who nominated St James the Greater as the first apostle to set foot in Europe, specifically at Iria Flavia, now El Padron, in Galicia. As a result, a certain amount of ill-feeling was generated at the Councils of Constance in 1417 and of Basle in 1434 convened to permit the rival bishops to argue their nation's case. No agreement was reached, but it was generally conceded that Joseph and his 150 disciples could not have crossed the Straits of Dover on the shirt of Josephes, the saint's son, as John of Glastonbury (c. 1400) tells us; and that the monastery at Glastonbury was founded not by Joseph in the first century, but by Celtic monks some time late in the fifth.

The history of the Christian Church in Roman Britain still remains as obscure as it is fascinating, and it can only be vaguely reconstructed from occasional references in the writings of our first historians, Gildas (516?–?570) and Bede (673–735). The venerable scholar of Jarrow has a curious story that one Lucius, 'a king of Britain', sent a letter to Pope Eleutherius in Rome praying that he might be made a Christian by rescript. His pious request was quickly granted, says Bede, after which Britain became a Christian state and remained so until the time of the Emperor Diocletian: that is, from c.180 to 305, when the persecutions began. This reign of terror, the tenth after Nero, lasted longer and was more cruel than any of the others and continued for ten years, marked by the burning of churches, the outlawing of innocent people, and the martyrdom of the faithful. Among the martyrs was St Alban – 'Illustrious Alban, faithful Britain's child', and two others, Aaron and Julius.[4] Of the three St Alban is the most important, for he is the protomartyr of the British Church and the only national saint with a continuous *cultus* from the fourth century. Moreover, despite the rather arguable details of his martyrdom as told by the mediaeval hagiographers, there are enough facts to substantiate the legend. We know, for instance, that St Germanus of Auxerre, one of the soldier-bishops who flourished in the fifth century, visited St Alban's tomb at Verulamium in 429, which was only some hundred years after the martyrdom, proving that there was an 'Albanus' who died for the faith. And so revered was this personage that Germanus exchanged some of his own precious relics (bones of the apostles) for some dust from the martyr's tomb.

A tomb and church, then, there must have been as early as 429, and Alban himself must have been revered enough to explain how his shrine became a place of pilgrimage for foreigners like St Germanus of Auxerre. Unfortunately we do not know who precisely this first British martyr was. Tradition says he was a Roman soldier who sheltered a Christian priest fleeing

[4] See *Bede's Ecclesiastical History of the English People.* Edited by Bertram Colgrave and R. A. B. Mynors. Oxford at the Clarendon Press, 1969. pp. 29–37.

from the authorities. The priest escaped, but Alban was apprehended and executed. But the story as told by Bede is based on an early account written by a Celtic monk whose world was inhabited by the sort of chimeras which we can still see staring out from the parapets of the mediaeval cathedrals. According to this holy man, when St Alban's head rolled from the block, it was accompanied by the headsman's eyeballs.

Such details, though anatomically interesting, do not tell us to what extent the Britons who watched the martyrdom of St Alban had accepted the Christian faith, and in the absence of any other written records, we are unable to say very much about this critical period in our religious history. But there is one contemporary observer who does give us a glimpse of what was going on. His name is Gildas, a British monk born early in the sixth century somewhere up north, perhaps in Strathclyde, and educated in Roman studies in a Welsh monastery, perhaps Bangor, the *alma mater* of Pelagius. After being married and widowed, Gildas travelled extensively all over Britain and Ireland. He was one of those Celtic religious who subjected themselves to a regime of extreme hardship in caves or on mountain sides. Gildas chose Flat Holme Island in the Bristol Channel for his hermitage and it might have been here that he wrote his splendid tract, *The Ruin of Britain*. At the end of his life he emigrated, or perhaps fled, to Brittany where he established a monastery at Rhuis on Morbihan Bay.

The Venerable Bede calls *The Ruin of Britain* 'a tearful discourse': in other words, it was a lament about a Britain which had lost its Christian faith, was too craven to fight for its existence, and too wicked to know right from wrong. This was the result, says Gildas:

> No sooner were the Romans gone than the Picts and Scots, like worms which in the heat of midday come forth from their holes, hastily landed again from their coracles in which they had been carried across the Irish Sea. These barbarians differed from one another in their customs, but were equally

> inspired with the same blood-lust, and much preferred to hide their villainous faces in hair rather than cover their private parts with decent clothing.* Moreover, having heard of the departure of our friends who had resolved never to return [i.e., the Romans], they ravaged the whole country on a wider scale than before right up to the Wall [Hadrian's Wall]. To oppose them a garrison was mustered to defend the Wall, but they turned out to be a cowardly, useless, and finally panic-stricken company. As a result, many of them were dragged from atop the Wall and battered to death. Now men abandoned the Wall altogether, left their cities, and fled. The barbarians hunted them down relentlessly and butchered them like sheep. . .[5]

After this, continues Gildas in his characteristic style:

> desolation spread over nearly all the land till at last its red and savage tongue licked the coasts of the western sea. Towns were levelled to the ground with battering rams; farmers, priests, and their congregations were slaughtered and even burnt by the barbarians. Coping-stones and battlements, altars and columns, corpses still bleeding, were all piled together in the middle of the ruined towns, as in a horrible wine-press. Burial there was none, save under the ruins of houses or in the maw of some beast of prey. Only the few who had fled to the mountains, there on the tops of precipitous cliffs, or in the depths of impenetrable forests, succeeded in dragging out a life truly precarious and full of terrors.[6]

Thus the angry old monk describes the end of Romano-British society and, with it, the Christian Church which had

* This must surely refer to the Scottish kilt.

[5] *The Works of Gildas, surnamed 'Sapiens', or the Wise.* Edited by J. A. Giles. London: George Bell & Sons, 1908. p. 307.

[6] *Ibid.*, pp. 308–12.

taken hold to some extent among Romanized Britons. The collapse of this society followed the arrival of the Saxon invaders. The *lux aeterna* that Christianity had shed on this remote province 'on the edge of the habitable globe' seemed extinguished for ever. Only in a few obscure corners of these islands could there now be found ministers of this light. Elsewhere new gods appeared on the scene, gods with hideous attributes and barbarous names, the gods of the Saxon invaders. The splendid or powerful or beautiful divinities of the Romans together with the rustic deities of the pagan Celts had gone for ever and nobody would ever again worship Mithras or Nodens in Britain. The gods had become ghosts.

For a long time, however, their shrines and sanctuaries survived, especially in rural places. The strongest concentration of these sanctuaries is found in and around Hadrian's Wall, though all we usually know about the god memorialized in such cases is his name inscribed on an altar or dedicatory tablet. It would seem that such godlings were really only the good luck mascots of serving regiments and had about as much spiritual authority as charms and amulets.

In southern Britain, always more peaceful and prosperous than the North, the most revered pagan gods were given proper, if miniscule, temples. One such temple dating from 300 BC lies under the runways of the London airport; another, dedicated to Ororiouth, a god (goddess?) evidently associated with women's diseases, under a housing site in Welwyn, Herfordshire. Christian sanctuaries, in contrast, are much rarer. In fact, the slowness of the Romano-Britons to accept Christianity even after all other cults had been proscribed by the proclamation of Constantine, has long puzzled historians; and evidence of the British aristocracy's unwillingness to oust the old gods is seen in the mosaics on the floors of one or two luxurious villas like Lullingstone in Kent in which representations of the classical themes – Bellerophon on his winged steed, Neptune accompanied by dolphins – have not been defaced, as one would expect, but have simply had the Christian chi-rho monogram added. Though frowned on by the Church Fathers and banished by the legislators, the old gods died hard.

BATH (Avon): the Temple of Sulis

Guidebook: *The City of Bath: Official Guide*. Bath City Council. Latest edition.

The Roman *Aquae Sulis* was sacred to a Celtic divinity who undoubtedly had a shrine at this celebrated spa long before the Romans arrived in AD 45. We know so little about this Sulis, Sul, or Sol that this particular deity is referred to by some authorities as 'he', by others as 'she'. 'She' seems more likely in that the Romans identified Sulis, Sul, or Sol with Minerva; they erected a magnificent temple near the sacred spring in Bath in honour of *Sul-Minerva*.

It was this spring issuing from the ground at a temperature of 120°F. which made Aquae Sulis of such special importance to the Romans. The visitor will see from the excellent models and plans laid out in the Museum the extent to which the warm spring was exploited, both for religious and pleasurable purposes. The spa must have become a resort of exceptional importance, with all manner of entertainments provided for the tourists, though the first task of a visitor was to pray at the sacred spring itself and to worship at the altar of the deity. The many offerings thrown into the spring and recovered during recent excavations tell their own story – 3000 coins, six pewter vessels, and twenty 'curse tablets' of which this one is typical:

> May the person who stole Vilbia from me be liquefied! Whoever devoured her is a brute, whether it was Velvinna, Exsupereus, Verianus, Severinus, Augustalis, Comitianus, Catusminianus, Germanilla, or Jovina.

Curses like this written in Vulgar Latin show how semi-literate were many – perhaps most – of the Britons who

16 The abbey seen behind the Great Bath reminds us that Aquae Sulis was also a religious centre in Roman times, with a temple dedicated to the Celtic goddess Sul, identified with Minerva.

frequented the shrine. At the same time, the Romans took care to keep up the standards of the temple by the appointment of special clergy. We actually have the name of one of them, L. Marcius Memor, a *haruspex*, or augurer. One wonders what branch of divination this priest specialized in, whether the standard Roman practice of examining sheeps' livers for omens, or the Celtic system based on the flight, cries, and defecations of birds.

There could be no greater proof of the popularity of Aquae Sulis throughout the northern provinces of the Empire than the dedicatory inscriptions left by visitors from overseas. A certain 'Priscus' from Chartres came, so did 'Peregrinus' from Trier, and 'Rusonia Aventina' from Metz. And if further evidence of the shrine's wealth and prosperity were needed, we have the ruins of thirty or more villas clustered within a ten-mile radius of the town which grew up around the sacred precincts. With its villas, farms, industries, and main roads linking it with all the major towns of Britain, Aquae Sulis helped the whole western region of Britain to prosper until the end of the occupation. Even so, there are signs that the spa was beginning to fall on hard times even before the Irish pirates from the west and Saxon raiders from the east began to harass and plunder the province.

During the fourth century the baths were still being improved, but sometime early in the fifth century the spring got out of control, there was serious flooding, and the foundations of the entire complex of temple, baths, and hostels were threatened. The spa now became so marshy that it was practically uninhabitable; and soon after Aquae Sulis, an example of provincial elegance, disappeared from the records, apart from one last reference to it in an eighth-century poem called *The Ruin*:

> Splendid was this city which the Fates destroyed.
> Its monuments have fallen: the work of giants moulders away.

The roofs collapse, the towers are in ruins. . .
Though the city wall, now gray with moss, withstood
The assaults of king after king, and was unshaken by storms,
Now its massive gate has fallen,
And the hot springs which filled its many baths are lost. . . .[7]

But thanks to the excavations undertaken at Bath since the restoration of the town in the eighteenth century, much of the Roman site has been revealed, notably the sequence of actual baths which tell us about the Romans' preoccupation with this form of social intercourse; for we see that, not content with hot and cold plunge baths, swimming baths, and Turkish baths, they installed sauna baths with accompanying rest rooms where bathers could have a massage and a pleasant nap. A great deal of this elaborate establishment can still be seen by the visitor. Otherwise, only odds and ends of the temple have been found, the most striking artefact of all being the Medusa head which adorned the façade of the Temple.

LONDON: the Temple of Mithras
Guidebook: *The London Mithraeum*. H. M. Stationery Office. Latest edition.

This is the best preserved of the five Mithraic shrines found in Britain. It was also probably the most important of the British centres of this cult, as London was pre-eminent almost from the beginning of the Roman occupation. The present site of the Mithraeum is in Temple Court, Queen Victoria Street, but the building itself was originally nearby on the east bank of the Walbrook River, now confined within a tunnel like its companion stream, the Fleet.

The reconstructed Mithraeum will give the visitor a fair idea

[7] Paraphrased translation by James Wellard of *The Ruin* from *Three Old English Elegies*. Edited by R. F. Leslie. Manchester University Press, 1961. pp. 51–2.

17 Mithras, worshipped throughout the Roman Empire principally by army officers and wealthy merchants, sacrifices a bull in the ceremony known as the *taurobolium*. Penitents were bespattered with the bull's blood in a form of baptism which gave the promise of eternal life.

of what the meeting places of this oriental cult were like, for he will be able to see the general lay-out, a very important factor if one wishes to understand the powerful hold the Mithraic religion had on its devotees. The London site does not, however, fully demonstrate how mysterious were these sacred places, which originally were located in caves and grottoes. For Mithraism had a direct connection with the most ancient of all religions, nature-worship, the primeval character of which can be seen in the Cave Art of the last Ice Age. By conducting their worship in subterranean temples built to resemble caves or grottoes, the devotees of Mithras were the direct descendants of cavemen who performed their rites in real caverns, or of the later forest-dwellers who worshipped in sacred groves where priests dressed in the skins of wild animals bespattered stone altars with sacrificial blood. And so powerful was the spell of the ancient belief that even in such civilized surroundings as Roman London, the initiation ceremonies held in the 'cave' must have had a profound effect on the neophyte who, having first passed across the vestibule of the temple, descended into the crypt where he beheld in the brilliantly lit grotto the icon of Mithras in the act of slaying the bull, the image surrounded by lion-headed statues and other symbolic monsters. He would also be aware of worshippers half-hidden in the shadows, kneeling in prayer on their stone benches. And in this solemn, fear-invoking atmosphere, he would celebrate baptism and communion, the former a ceremony of purification in which the devotee was almost touched on the forehead with a red-hot iron; the latter a partaking of the sacramental bread and wine. The neophyte was then required to prepare himself for fellowship by fasting and abstinence. All these activities, and particularly the initiation ceremonies, were to excite the derision of the Christian Fathers who are our principal source of the cult's secrets. Saint Augustine declares that during these ceremonies some of the congregation in bird-masks stood about flapping artificial wings and croaking away, while others roared like lions. By participating in some such rites, many senior army officers, administrators, and rich merchants dedicated themselves to a god who, they believed, fought for the triumph of good over evil, who was the champion of truth and justice, whose name was never called upon in vain, and who awaited those who lived in righteousness as their Father in Heaven.

Something of the solemnity of this stern religion can be felt in the Mithraeum in Victoria Street whose endless bustle and commercialism are about as far removed from the mysteries of worship in grottoes as one can imagine, though the Mithraeum itself was a sophisticated structure, with no superficial resemblance to a natural cave. The reconstruction of the London temple shows that the shrine contained a central nave, two aisles, and an apse for the statuary. The visitor will notice how the entrance threshold has been worn away by the feet of the congregation, and if he then visits the London Museum where the collection of the Mithraic finds are housed, he will see how wealthy these worshippers were. The exhibits include the unique stone slab depicting the *taurobolium*, or slaying of the bull by Mithras, and several of the finest statues ever found in Roman Britain, including a marble head of Mithras in his Phrygian cap, a figure of Mercury, a head of Minerva, and the marvellous head of Serapis, the Graeco-Egyptian god, regarded by his devotees as the ruler of the universe. All these statues were imported from Italy and perhaps sculpted in Greek workshops. They illustrate the extent to which Britain had become part of the classical world.

LULLINGSTONE (Kent): the Christian Chapel

Guidebook: *Lullingstone Roman Villa*. London: Ministry of Works Guide.

Lullingstone is within easy reach of London, on the west bank of the River Darent, about five miles north of Sevenoaks, and though only some thirty miles or so from Charing Cross in a heavily built-up area, the Kentish countryside hereabouts manages to retain something of the rural character and beauty of the England of Chaucer and even of Roman Britain. The Darent flows through a rich agricultural valley, which explains why the whole region is dotted with the relics of Roman farm-buildings, including four villas, of which Lullingstone is the most famous.

The original villa was built late in the first century, soon after the conquest and eventual pacification of the south. The site had all the advantages needed for successful farming. The

18 Six *orantes*, or Christian worshippers with hands raised in prayer, were painted on the wall of the Christian chapel in a Roman villa at Lullingstone in Kent.

ground was fertile; the nearby River Darent afforded water for all the irrigation that might be required; and the prehistoric forests had been largely cleared away by generations of British farmers. In such an almost perfect rural setting, some rich man, perhaps a senior Roman official, was bound to build a house from which to supervise his estate; and this house, in turn, was quickly enlarged and beautified until it ended up as a classical villa of the sort found throughout the length and breadth of the Roman world – from Africa to Britain.

The estate was worked by slaves, probably hundreds of them being needed to cultivate the fields and orchards, together with the many specialists required for a farm which was totally self-supporting. The flocks and herds raised on a Roman estate of this type were far larger than will be found on a modern English farm, for the cattle, sheep, and pigs had vast areas to feed on at no cost to their owners. The herdsmen and shepherds who tended them were provided with all the food they wanted and were no doubt given help by the estate carpenters and masons to build a home for themselves within sight of the 'big house'.

That a Roman building stood here at Lullingstone has been obvious since the seventeenth century on account of the artefacts which were constantly being turned up by the plough. Then excavations began in 1949, continued for twelve years, and are now completed, leaving the site systematically laid out and presented so that a guide is unnecessary.

The main exhibits at the site are the paintings and mosaics found during the excavations. One of the mosaics was discovered in a room evidently dedicated to the worship of a water-goddess. It depicted three water-nymphs, of which two survive. But the paramount interest and importance of Lullingstone is undoubtedly its Christian shrine, or house-chapel. The archaeologists picked out from the debris fragments of painted plaster which, when pieced together, made up a frieze of six human figures wearing flowing tunics with long sleeves, the characteristic robes of the Roman and Romanized gentry of the fourth century. Two of the figures have the wide, deep-set eyes typical of Roman portraiture. The Orante posture – that is, the supplicant standing with arms outstretched – is inseparable from early Christian tradition.

The six praying figures and the painting on another wall of the chi-rho symbol are positive evidence that the Lullingstone villa was at one time a Christian home. Before that it was obviously a pagan household, whence the splendid mosaics of typical classical myths, one of the abduction of Europa by Zeus in the guise of a bull; another of Bellerophon astride the winged-horse Pegasus killing the Chimaera. But whoever the owners of this villa were during the three hundred years of its existence, they certainly belonged to the Romano-British aristocracy, judging by the luxuriousness of this mansion, with its mosaic floors, wall paintings, central heating, baths, and mausoleum. Their status may also account for the Christian house-chapel, converted from an older pagan room, for one can assume that in Roman Britain during the latter half of the fourth century Christianity became the religion of the landed gentry. Such important people would, from expediency, be among the first to adopt the new religion when it became quasi-official by the Edict of Milan in AD 313. But Christians seem to have remained a fairly exclusive group who worshipped not in churches, but in their own homes. The implication is that Christianity was not widespread in fourth-century Britain, even though the Roman army had actually been ordered to recite a prayer to the Christian god. In fact, despite this imperial behest, the officers went on attending their Mithraic lodges; the soldiers paid lip-homage to their various mascot-type gods; and not a single Christian church or shrine was built in any military installation anywhere in Britain. There were, however, fifty-eight known pagan temples on the Wall alone!

[5]
THE GROANS OF THE BRITONS

To Aetius, thrice Consul.
Subject: The Groans of the Britons:
an appeal for help.

The barbarians drive us into the sea,
the sea throws us back on the barbarians.
Two kinds of death await us: we are
either slain or drowned.

Gildas, *The Ruin of Britain*, ch. 20

In a letter written about the year 480, Sidonius Apollinaris, bishop of Clermont in Gaul, described the barbarians who were about to conquer and colonize the Roman province of Britannia in these words:

> They give the impression that every member of the crew in their high-prowed ships is the captain, so accustomed are all of them both to issue and to obey orders, to teach and to learn piracy. As an enemy, they are unsurpassed in brutality. They attack without warning, but when sighted, slip away. Shipwreck, far from terrifying them, is an exercise in seamanship. They gladly endure the danger of a rock-bound coast if it enables them to achieve surprise. Moreover, when it is time to set sail for home, it is their custom on the evening of their departure to sacrifice one in ten of their prisoners by drowning or crucifixion. Such is the nature of their religion.[1]

This contemporary description of the Saxon raids is about the nearest we get to an eyewitness account of what was

[1] Sidonius Apollinaris, Bishop of Clermont. *Letters*. Book viii, vi, 14–5. Translated by James Wellard. London: Heinemann, 1936. 65.

happening to Britain in the fifth century, for we have no British source for the period. Our first national historians were all monks and wrote in the comparative security of their monasteries: Gildas (c. 550) at Ruis in France, Bede (c. 730) at Jarrow, England, and Nennius (c. 800) at Bangor, Wales, were more concerned with the wickedness of the world than with actual events, and this makes it difficult to evaluate their works. Nennius, for instance, who is the first historian to mention Arthur, 'the last of the Romans' and the first of our national heroes, strains belief by stating that this British general, wrongly called a king, personally slew 960 of the Saxon enemy at the Battle of Mons Badonis. And even *The Anglo-Saxon Chronicle*, begun around AD 893 at the behest of King Alfred, relies heavily upon legend for the years between AD 450 and AD 730, the twilight period of Roman Britannia. The reason is simple: the invaders who destroyed the province – the Angles, Saxons, Jutes, and Frisians – were illiterate and left no written records of their invasions and conquests.

Without any literary sources, then, we have to fall back on the occasional observations of foreign writers or the findings of archaeology. Archaeology is our principal source of information, since the invading barbarians left their treasure, as well as their bones, buried all over southern and eastern England. The nineteenth-century antiquarians dug indiscriminately into hundreds of their graves, but unfortunately the historical evidence of their excavations was largely negative, even if the provincial museums acquired a great many artefacts, most of them pertaining to war. Even now, about all that we can confidently say concerning this twilight period of our history is that England was roughly divided down the middle into two nations, the eastern side of this imaginary frontier occupied by small groups of German invaders turned colonists; the western side by nuclei of Romano-British refugees.

Who, then, were these last 'Romans' who clung to the old Mediterranean life-style in the valleys of the West Country and the mountains of Wales? Some of them were undoubtedly members of the native aristocracy – owners of villas and large estates, administrators, civil servants, and rich businessmen. Two of these survivors appear as larger-than-life figures out of the mists – Ambrosius Aurelianus and Arturius (Arthur) who, as commanders-in-chief of armies trained in the fashion of the legions, kept western Britain 'Roman' for a hundred years. 'Roman' at this period meant quasi-Christian, in contrast to the heathenism of the German invaders who were now battering at the gates of Rome itself. For the Christian Church throughout what was left of civilized Europe had inherited the authority of the Roman senate and actually undertook the task of defending the remnants of the Empire on the field of battle.

Yet paradoxically, the Church condoned and even extolled those pacifists who rejected outright all civic duties and retired to the deserts and rock-bound islands, an abdication of responsibility which disgusted old-fashioned Romans, a few of whom still survived in a world where political power was firmly in the hands of the Christian hierarchs. One of these survivors was Zosimus, a Greek historian who lived and worked in Constantinople in the second half of the fifth century AD. Zosimus held the office of chancellor of the imperial exchequer and, as a government official, no doubt kept his pagan and therefore quasi-subversive beliefs to himself, as did his more famous successor, Procopius. But in his so-called *New History* written in the privacy of his home, the chancellor gives us more than a hint of what a Roman of the old order felt about men who elected to 'drop out' – those who in his day were called 'monks' or 'the solitary ones' (μοναχοὶ). In a passage which obviously deeply influenced Gibbon, he expresses his indignation thus:

> The Christian Church was then filled with those men whom they call Monks. These are persons who abstain from lawful marriage and who fill large colleges in many cities and villages with able-bodied and unmarried men unwilling to contribute military or any other service to the commonwealth. These men by their arts have acquired possession of

> extensive lands and under the pretext of charity to the poor have, I might say, almost reduced other citizens to beggary.[2]

It was the ascetics' attitude towards marriage which appalled Zosimus who was frankly bewildered by the Christian detestation of sex which, as Gibbon remarks, meant that 'desire was imputed as a crime, and marriage was tolerated as a defect'. The Gallic-Roman, Claudius Rutilius Namatianus, ex-prefect of Rome, joins in. 'What sort of men are they who deliberately seek to make themselves wretched?' he asks while returning home in 416 AD to his estate in Aquitaine and observing from the prow of his ship the barren islands off the coast of north-western Italy.

> Now, as we drift along,
> Capraria rises out of the sea. Squalid the isle
> And filled with men who shun the light of day.
> Why do they wish to dwell alone observed by none?
> What madness afflicts them to reject everything good
> Because they fear evil?[3]

Rutilius could just as well have been asking these questions of British hermits perched on rocks in the Bristol Channel. And the answer would have surprised him: many of these ascetics – and this was certainly true of the British hermits who were to be known as the Celtic saints – turned out to be the ultimate conservers of civilization in northern Europe, leaving for posterity not only the example of their holiness, but later, through the labours of their disciples in the monasteries which sprang up around their cells, the heritage of the classical world.

So if we want to know something of the story of the end of Roman Britain, we must look to those forests and rocky islets of the west where the solitary ones lived. Our first historian,

[2] *The History of Count Zosimus*. London: J. Davis, 1814. p. 150.

[3] *De Reditu Suo*. Translated by J. F. Savage-Armstrong. London: George Bell, 1907. pp. 145–7.

Gildas, was one of them. He chose for his hermitage Flat Holme Island in the Bristol Channel, a storm-swept rock half a mile long by half a mile wide. His colleague, St Samson, squatted on one of the uninhabited Scilly Islands still known by his name. St David, another contemporary, is associated with an unidentified rock off the Welsh coast where he shared a hermitage with St Paulinus who had become blind with much weeping over the sins of mankind. St Conan clambered up Roche Rock near St Austell in Cornwall and established his hermitage in a cleft of the pinnacle. The ruined chapel built into the rock is on the site of the hermit's cell (see the jacket illustration). Not far away, St Gudwal commandeered an islet somewhere off Penzance, and many other ascetics abjured the world, the flesh, and the devil in caves and caverns around our shores. It is still incredible how they could have survived under such conditions, but perhaps we should not take too literally the stories of their ordeals as told by the mediaeval hagiographers who seem to have a predilection for the bizarre. The biographer of St Nectan of Devon, for instance, credits the holy man with walking half a mile to his cave in the forest carrying his head under his arm. It was these Celtic 'athletes of Christ' who played a major role in the next phase of our island's history, a role far more important than that of the tribal chieftains like Arthur who set up independent kingdoms in western Britain, for the communities which sprang up around the hermitages of the saints were to become the centres of national and even international power, the great abbeys of the Dark and Middle Ages.

The number of religious houses established in the fifth and sixth centuries is remarkable; several hundreds of them are listed in the *Ordnance Survey of Dark Age Britain*. One of them at Bangor Iscoed in South Wales is said by Bede to have housed over 2000 monks. How, one wonders, were all these inmates fed, let alone occupied? According to Gildas, many of them did very little other than eat and drink to excess. Britain, he says, had become a land of false monks and shameless priests – a charge which some five hundred years later was to be levelled at the brothers of the very monastery he founded at Saint Gildas-de-Ruis in Brittany, the monastery to which Peter Abelard was assigned as abbot in 1125. In a letter to Héloise, her lover describes the abbey in words which echo the indictment of the British brethren by Gildas:

> I am living in a land of barbarians whose very language is incomprehensible and revolting. The only people I meet are like wild beasts. The monks have never even known what a monastic rule is. And you should see my house! You would never believe that this is an abbey. The entrances are littered with the carcasses of deer, wolves, bears, and wild pigs. . . . Every day I undergo new dangers and any moment expect to see a sword dangling over my head.[4]

Abelard was not exaggerating. The monks tried both fire and poison to drive him out, and eventually succeeded. He had to flee by boat from that inhospitable land, a land which had been the second homeland of British monks like SS Illtud, Gildas, Samson, Patrick, and David.

It is through the *Lives* of these sometimes famous, sometimes obscure, Celtic saints rather than in the occasional references of a Greek historian like Zosimus that we catch a glimpse of events in the last days of Roman Britain. St Patrick, the Apostle of Ireland, is an excellent example, for here we have a Briton who tells us in his autobiography (the *Confessio*) what life was like in Britannia in the fifth century. Patrick was born a 'Roman', his father being a *decurio* (town councillor) with a country estate near the mouth of the River Severn: i.e., in that part of the province which remained Roman the longest. Before he was captured by Irish pirates and carried away as a slave, he must have gone to school long enough to learn to read and write in what he calls 'the language of mankind' – Latin; and though his

[4] *The Letters of Abelard and Héloise*. Translated from the Latin by C. K. Scott Moncrieff. London: Guy Chapman, 1925. p. 178.

use of that language is inelegant and even at times rustic (in comparison with Gauls like Rutilius whose Latin was almost Virgilian), what he has to say is full of interest. He tells us that the safe and orderly life his grandparents had known, a time when a traveller could go freely and safely from Bannavem Tabernae (where Patrick was born) a thousand miles to Rome along paved roads the entire way, that such a time was gone. Now the pirates crossed the seas with impunity and carried off Britons and sold them into slavery. Yet in Patrick's day Britain is still part of the Roman Empire, and he is a Roman citizen, and as such he expects to be treated with respect, especially by barbarians. Obviously the Latin mentality survived even after the Romans had gone; and it survived largely because so much had been left intact – a prosperous country, an efficient agriculture, useful industries, first-class communications, well-organized national and local services, and above all, a concept of law and order. Added to these accompaniments of civilized living, a highly efficient system of national defence was available to the natives if they had had the energy and will to make use of it – four legionary fortresses located at strategic points throughout southern Britain, scores of military camps, and a system of naval stations all along the Saxon shore. It was true that the professional administrators and troops had gone, and with them many of the national leaders, wealthy merchants, and skilled craftsmen. Perhaps this was why the natives, now leaderless and unused to fending for themselves, did not make proper use of the resources left them and resisted the continual invasions so feebly. The Roman Channel Fleet, which had admittedly had great trouble even in its heyday in fighting off the pirates, was withdrawn altogether. Without the Roman army and navy, the Britons cried out for somebody to come and save them, appealing first to Rome, then to the semi-Romanized clan chieftains of Wales and north-west Britain.

They did, however, make one or two attempts to defend themselves. In 429, they were called to arms by St Germain, bishop of Auxerre, who was on an official visit at a time when the Britons were being harassed by both Picts and Scots. St Germain was typical of the new Christian hierarchs who had taken over the administration of the old provinces from the military governors. A soldier as well as a priest, Germain quickly organized the demoralized natives into a militia and finally led them himself to victory against the heathen. He had taught them to shout 'Alleluia' at the top of their lungs as they charged – an early example of psychological warfare.

Twenty years later, another military leader appeared on the scene, a nobleman called Ambrosius Aurelianus who was followed by Arthur as commander-in-chief of a national army trained in the Roman fashion and making special use of heavy cavalry – the mail-clad horsemen who were the prototypes of the mediaeval knights. While Aurelianus and Arthur were in the field against the fierce but ill-disciplined barbarians, Britain remained 'Roman'.

But despite the inspiration of a soldier-bishop like Germain and the last stands made by the legendary heroes, the system finally collapsed. Neither Roman discipline nor Christian faith were enough. It was as though the people no longer had either the will or the incentive to resist. Most of them, after all, had been slaves or serfs throughout the Roman occupation, and to a farm-worker it could not have made much difference who owned the great mansion with its centrally-heated rooms, baths, mosaics, and imported luxuries.

Indifference to nationhood is what some commentators assume was the reason for what the first of our historians and the commentator nearest to the time calls 'The Ruin of Britain'. But Gildas blames the tyrannical rulers, corrupt ministers, and false priests for the collapse which was bound to end in some form of dictatorship. And, as if on cue, a 'strong man' did emerge from the unconquered but semi-Romanized clans of Wales, a king called Vortigern whose first act was to invite in as allies the traditional enemies of Britain. The arrival in Kent sometime around AD 455 of the Saxon chieftains, Hengist and Horsa, marks the nominal end of Roman Britain.

Yet England was still too big and forested a land for small bands of raiders to conquer and administer. And those Roman Britons who did escape the Saxon invaders and the Irish pirates could survive for a time in a country whose woods abounded in game, its seas and rivers with fish, while those who lived in walled cities were in no particular danger, since the Saxons knew nothing of siege warfare. The cities, in fact, seem simply to have been abandoned, and the countryside supervised from the magnificent villas left deserted.

By the end of the fifth century it was becoming difficult to live in a civilized fashion. There was no recognized government, no established law and order, not even a common language and coinage. The actual end is described by the Venerable Bede, who must have talked with the sons and grandsons of men who had witnessed the final cataclysm. Bede, like his fellow-monk Gildas, was conditioned to see all human calamities as a consequence of divine justice, so we have no way of telling whether he was exaggerating the disaster. But this is how he says it was:

> The fire kindled by the hands of the heathen executed the just vengeance of God on the nation for its crimes. . . . Public and private buildings fell in ruins, priests were everywhere slain at their altars, prelates and people alike perished by sword and fire, and there was no one left to bury those who had died a cruel death. Some of the miserable remnant were captured in the mountains and butchered indiscriminately; others, exhausted by hunger, came forward and submitted themselves to the enemy, ready to accept perpetual slavery for the sake of food; some fled sorrowfully to lands beyond the sea, while those who remained led a wretched existence in fear and dread among the mountains and woods and precipitous rocks.[5]

[5] *Bede's Ecclesiastical History of the British People.* Edited by Bertram Colgrave and R.A.B. Mynors. Oxford: Clarendon Press, 1969. p. 53.

19 The fort of Vercovicium (Housesteads) about midway along Hadrian's Wall is an excellent example of Roman military architecture. Facilities included a hospital, baths, special quarters for officers, barracks for the men, and a latrine, shown here.

VERCOVICIUM – Housesteads (Cumbria): a Roman Fort

Guidebook: Breeze, David John, *Hadrian's Wall*, maps, plans. Harmondsworth: Penguin, 1978.

Vercovicium is the best preserved and excavated of sixteen major forts situated along the 115 miles of the great northern defence system known as Hadrian's Wall.

It is on account of this stupendous monument that the

Emperor Hadrian (Publius Aelius Hadrianus, AD 76–138) is the Roman most identified with British history. He came to Britain in 121 because the northern tribes were continually in revolt, and after considering the possible alternatives, he decided to build a wall across the country to separate the Caledonian barbarians from the civilized Britons. This was the first time the Romans had used a fixed frontier system, except in Upper Germany where Hadrian had erected a wooden palisade, considered adequate even in that wild country. But Britain was, and always had been, one of the most intractable of the provinces, requiring four legions to police it despite its small area. Africa, twenty times as large, needed only one legion. Hadrian decided, therefore, to release the pressure on the army by building a barrier of stone, and so began to erect his Wall in

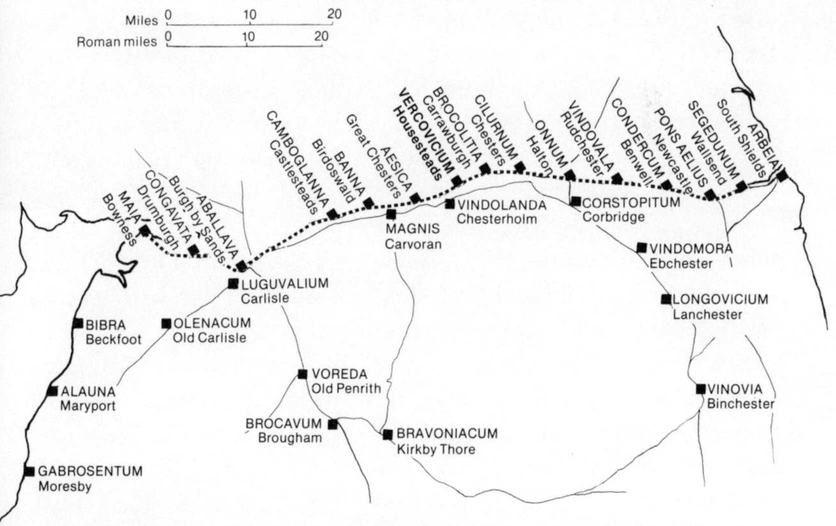

20 Drawing showing the main features of Hadrian's Wall. The Wall was commissioned by Emperor Hadrian in 122 to act as a frontier between the barbarian tribes of northern England and their potential allies in southern Scotland. Stretching from coast to coast, it required 15,000 auxiliaries to man its forts, milecastles, and look-out turrets.

122, finishing it four years later in 126. The barrier was designed to be fifteen feet high plus battlements. On the northern side of the Wall ran a V-shaped ditch twenty-seven feet wide and eight feet deep. About every mile a square fortlet was erected, with three intermediate watch-towers. Housesteads (Vercovicium), about midway along the defence line, was chosen for the site of a full-scale legionary fort covering fifty acres. These forts were the permanent barracks and headquarters of the legions on foreign service and represent in microcosm, as it were, the mind as well as the organization of the Roman army, and the visitor will have no difficulty in seeing why at Housesteads: the barracks, baths, granary, hospital, and latrines tell the story. The last of these installations are sited in a rectangular building provided with two rows of seats placed over sewers which were regularly flushed from lead-lined tanks. A water channel for cleansing the sponges which the Romans used in place of toilet-paper and a basin at the lavatory's exit for washing hands have also survived. The arrangement typifies the Roman concern with hygiene and the determination, even on the frontiers of civilization, to maintain the highest standards of sanitation.

We can see, too, what a Roman army hospital was like. The clinic at Housesteads is extremely well-designed. The doctors in military hospitals all over the Empire were probably more occupied with everyday medical cases than they were with war wounds; and no doubt they treated the local civilians for many of the same complaints we suffer from to-day, judging by the contemporary medical books. Here, for instance, is a description of a tonsillectomy:

> Having seated the patient in the sunlight and directed him to open his mouth, one assistant holds his head and another presses down the tongue with a tongue-depressor. We take a hook and perforate the tonsil with it and drag it outwards as much as we can without dragging the capsule out along with it; and then we cut it off at the root with the tonsillotome

(tonsil-knife) suited to that side, for there are two such instruments having opposite curvatures. After the excision of one tonsil, we may operate on the other in the same way.[6]

Special interest attaches to Vercovicium because of the civilian township which grew up on the south side of the fort. This kind of settlement was the prototype of the mediaeval English village which developed in some cases into a provincial town. The existence of these civilian settlements or *vici* all along Hadrian's Wall suggests that the relations between the Romans, the Britons, and the barbarian Picts on the northern side of the barrier were not always unfriendly. It is probable that there was a considerable trade between the occupied and unoccupied zones and that Roman civilization was familiar to the inhabitants of the farthest north. It is difficult otherwise to understand how Christianity spread so rapidly – even to the remotest of the Isles – unless it is conceded that when the Christian missionaries came among the natives, they were respected as emissaries of Rome. And even though the Caledonian tribes had never surrendered to the legions, they were well aware of the might of Empire.

CANDIDA CASA (Wigtown, Scotland): the First Scottish Monastery

Guidebook: *Official Guide Book to Whithorne and Kirkmadrine.* London: Ministry of Works. Latest edition.

The first and one of the greatest monasteries of Dark Age Britain was founded early in the fifth century by Ninian, the Apostle of Scotland. But despite his obvious importance as a missionary, we have surprisingly little information about Ninian, the Venerable Bede supplying most of what we do have. He

[6] Paulus Aegineta, *The Medical Works.* Translated by F. Adams. London: The Sydenham Society, 1844–7. Book VI, Chapter XXX.

refers to him as 'a most revered bishop and holy man of the British nation who had been regularly instructed at Rome in the faith and mysteries of the truth'. On his return from Rome, Ninian brought with him some skilled stone-masons and with their help built the monastery called The White House, the first stone church to be erected in Scotland; and it was from this Candida Casa that Ninian and his monks set out to convert the Picts.

According to a mediaeval account, The White House was built on an island called *Witerne*, now the Isle of Whithorn, south east of Wigtown, Scotland, in a region remarkable for its hillforts, standing stones, and Pictish lake dwellings. Modern scholars, on the other hand, believe that the monastery was located in the royal burgh of Whithorn, so it is not certain which of the two places, the island or the town, is the actual site of a shrine once so revered that it was visited by most of the kings of Scotland, including Robert the Bruce and Mary Queen of Scots. On the Isle of Whithorn are the ruins of a small thirteenth-century chapel said to mark the actual site of St Ninian's monastery. Yet some of the oldest Christian monuments ever found in Britain were discovered in the ruins of the twelfth-century priory in Whithorn itself, notably the 'Latinus' tombstone which is in debased Latin and probably dates from the time of St Ninian. Some argue that if this stone was in its original position, Candida Casa was on the site of the priory in Whithorn and not on the island. The wording of the monument is puzzling. It reads: *We, Latinus aged 35 and his daughter aged 5, praise thee, O Lord. The grandsons of Barrovad erected this monument.*

Further along this Solway coast, about three miles west of the Isle of Whithorn just round Burrow Head, is a third site associated with the Apostle of Scotland and still called St Ninian's Cave. This cleft in the rocks was obviously occupied by Christian hermits, perhaps even monks from the White House. A number of inscribed stones carved with crosses of an early Christian date were found in this cave, together with a skeleton doubled up with its skull between the legs.

It can be seen that this trio of sacred sites – the Isle of Whithorn, the town of Whithorn itself, and the cave – suggests very strongly that whether St Ninian's White House was located here or not, south-western Caledonia was the birthplace of the Scottish Church which still commemorates its first apostle on September 16 each year.

LLANTWIT MAJOR (Glamorgan, Wales): an Early Welsh Monastery

Just as the Candida Casa of St Ninian was the premier monastery of Scotland, so Llantwit Major, the religious house founded by St Illtud, was the cradle of Welsh Christianity.

St Illtud is another of the very early Celtic saints whose life, like the times he lived in, is half-legendary. The earliest reference to him is in a seventh-century biography of St Samson who, along with SS Paul, David, and Gildas, is said to have been his pupil at the monastic school of Llanilltud *Fawr*, that is, 'the Great'. 'This Illtud,' says St Samson's biography, 'was the most learned of all the Britons both in the Old and New Testaments and in all kinds of philosophy – poetry and rhetoric, grammar and arithmetic'.[7] This learned man was born in Brecknock, south-east Wales, about the middle of the fifth century, and like other 'Romans' of the West Country, he travelled extensively, at one time as a soldier in the service of a Welsh king. He married a lady called Trynihid, but on the advice of an angel deserted her to become a hermit. Like all the gurus who lived in caves or forest shacks, Illtud attracted sightseers, then disciples; and since the land where he squatted was good and his followers worked hard, the community flourished and the foundations of the famous monastery and school were laid during his lifetime.

Unfortunately not a stone of St Illtud's monastery survives,

[7] J. H. Doble, *St Illtut*. Cardiff: Univ. of Wales, 1944. p. 32.

so that the visitor to Llantwit, eight miles south-east of Bridgend in Glamorgan, Wales must rely on his own observations and imagination to see this place as the spiritual capital of what was left of Roman Britain in the mid fifth century. However, the Vale of Glamorgan provides at least two good examples of Roman villas, one at Ely near Cardiff, the other near Llantwit Major. The latter was a large mansion containing some thirty centrally heated rooms and a complete suite of baths, including a sauna room, or *sudatorium*. Legend has it that this villa was the birthplace of St Illtud; with its excellent accommodation it might have served as the site for his first monastery. If, however, St Illtud had his hermitage in Llantwit Major itself, the parish church, parts of which date from the thirteenth century, is probably built on the site of the actual monastery. Inside the church, within the west nave, can be seen the famous 'Samson Cross' dedicated to 'Illtet, Samson, and Ebisar'.

As for the monastery, we should not think of it as resembling the great institutions of the Middle Ages, for we know that the Celtic monks preferred to live in numerous scattered cells, meeting only for services in a communal church. The regimen was severe, if we can believe the report that St Illtud insisted on the monks yoking themselves to the plough in place of oxen; and the story that he drove away his own wife when this lady came to visit him suggests that celibacy was beginning to be strictly observed in British monasteries. But what makes Llantwit Major particularly important is that this Welsh settlement was a major centre of learning after the Roman rule had collapsed and that it was from here that scholars and evangelists went abroad to educate and convert the barbarian kings of northern Europe.

TINTAGEL (Cornwall): a Cornish Monastery

Guidebook: *Tintagel, on the Coast of North Cornwall. The Official Guide*. Ed. J. Burrow. Cheltenham/London, 1978.

Tintagel Head on the north coast of Cornwall is popularly known as the site of 'King Arthur's Castle'. There is, however, no archaeological evidence that Arthur, the 'last of the Romans', lived in this fortress. Nor is Tintagel the seat of King Mark, his queen Iseult, and her lover Tristan. But it is the site of one of Britain's first monasteries dating back to the fifth century. The outlines of a dozen or more cells can still be seen, the principal one said to have been the hermitage of St Gwen. We know nothing about this abbess except that she was one of hundreds of Celtic saints whose actual existence is only testified in the names of sundry Welsh and Cornish churches dedicated to their memory. St Gwen of Tintagel seems to have become confused with another saint: namely, Gwen or Wenn, mother of St David of Wales. This Welsh Gwen is also identified with St Gwen of Brittany whose statues in a number of Breton churches show her to have had three breasts, an anatomic peculiarity to which the local curés have always taken exception, despatching the offending simulacra to church attics or burying them in the ground, declaring that such images were 'not conducive to devotion'. A good example is still *in situ* in the Chapel of St Venec in the parish of Brasparts near Quimper, and it shows the saint's three children by one of her husbands, Fracan. The fact that Gwen had two husbands and children by both of them entitled her to the honorific 'Three-Breasted'. In cases where a woman had three husbands and three sets of children, she was called Four-Breasted. As far as we know, there are no records of Five-Breasted women.

There is some evidence that the two Gwens, she of Cornwall and she of Brittany, were one and the same person, for in common with other Celtic saints of the fifth and sixth centuries, she may have travelled back and forth between the two coun-

21 The stone walls in this photograph of Tintagel in Cornwall are said to demarcate the cells of the nuns who occupied a monastery established here in the fifth century. The site was originally the hermitage of St Gwen, Celtic saint and legendary mother of St David.

tries. Legend has it that she was captured by Saxon pirates in mid Channel, but managed to climb down the side of the ship and walk back to Brittany on the water.

What is left of her monastery on Tintagel Head can tell us little about her life and times, though excavations have revealed one or two important clues. One room of the monastery had a hypocaust for central heating and another room is thought to have been a scriptorium. There was also a garden nearby. So we can assume that the little community of nuns lived in some comfort and, indeed, elegance as compared with women on the subsistence farms of this storm-lashed coast of Cornwall. Evidently some of the congregation were employed copying manuscripts in the scriptorium, others tended the garden, and others undertook the necessary household tasks, all contributing to a reasonably civilized, if austere, life.

We do not know what happened to the Tintagel monastery, which was undoubtedly already abandoned when Reginald, earl of Cornwall and illegitimate son of Henry I, built the first castle on the headland around 1145. It was certainly in ruins by the time John Leland visited it in 1539, for he mentions a chapel dedicated to St Ulette (Juliot?) in whose cloisters sheep were grazing. The little hermitage was probably abandoned as the Saxons advanced westwards and many of the leaders of the Celtic Church emigrated to Brittany.

[6]

HEATHEN KINGS AND CHRISTIAN SAINTS

As for the kings of Wales, I leave the history of them to Caradoc of Lancarvan, my contemporary, as I do also the kings of the Saxons to William of Malmesbury and Henry of Huntingdon. But I advise them to be silent concerning the kings of the Britons, since they have not that book written in the British tongue which Walter, archdeacon of Oxford, brought out of Brittany, and which, being a true history, I have thus taken care to translate.

Final paragraph of
Geoffrey of Monmouth's
Historia Britonum

'She was the only lady that he continually served with fresh dishes and to whom he sent golden cups by his courtiers. On her he bestowed all his smiles and to her addressed all his discourse' writes Geoffrey of Monmouth. 'The husband discovering this fell into a great rage and retired from the court without taking leave. King Uther, therefore, commanded him to return back to court, to make him satisfaction for this affront. But Gorlois refused to obey, upon which the king was highly incensed and vowed he would destroy his country.'[1]

Who, then, are these people? And when did all this take place? According to Geoffrey, writing in the twelfth century with the aid of what he calls 'a very old book in the British [i.e., the Celtic] tongue', Uther was Uther Pendragon, king of all the Britons; Gorlois was the duke of Cornwall; and the lady, wife of

[1] *Old English Chronicles, Geoffrey of Monmouth's British History*, London: George Bell, 1908. pp, 244 ff.

Gorlois, was Igerna, 'the greatest beauty in all Britain'. The time was the mid fifth century AD when, says Geoffrey, Stonehenge was erected. Uther Pendragon now admitted that 'my passion for Igerna is such that I can have neither ease of mind nor health of body unless I possess her . . .' But this was difficult since Gorlois had barricaded himself in his castle at Dimilioc in Cornwall and shut up Igerna in the castle of Tintagel, which was considered impregnable. Uther was now in a state of extreme anguish, mad with passion, so his courtiers hurriedly summoned Merlin the magician to advise him how to 'accomplish his desire with respect to Igerna'. Merlin quickly resolved the problem. He told Uther, 'I will metamorphose you into the true semblance of Gorlois, and in this guise Igerna will joyfully admit you.'

And so it was. Uther, metamorphosed, arrived at twilight, easily gained entrance to the chamber of the greatest beauty in Britain, entertained her with artful and amorous discourses, and was refused nothing that he desired. 'The same night after a long dalliance,' Geoffrey continues, 'she conceived the most renowned Arthur whose heroic and wonderful actions have justly rendered his name famous to posterity'.

Such is the material which is available to the historian trying to chronicle the period between the end of Britannia in AD 450 and the creation of England under King Alfred in AD 892. The vaguely prurient story of Arthur's conception is obviously fictitious. Geoffrey's own contemporary, William of Newburgh, denounced him as 'having lied shamelessly and saucily'. Yet one can understand how natural it was for a twelfth-century historian to invent some such magician as Merlin, since magic, or miracle, was needed to explain the facts as well as the mysteries of post-Roman Britain – the campaigns of cavalry commanders like Aurelius and Arthur on the one hand and the existence of monuments like Stonehenge and Hadrian's Wall on the other. Whether Merlin was invented by the ancient Welsh bards or whether he was an actual person, we shall never know. He himself (in Geoffrey of Monmouth's *History*, for instance) claimed that his father was a Roman consul. Arthur, however, seems more credible: he is mentioned in the eighth-century history of Nennius as the British commander who defeated the Saxon invaders at twelve named battles, the last of which, Mount Badon (Mons Badonicus), has all the hallmarks of being a recognizable historical event.

But, notwithstanding the minutiae of concrete evidence contained in the fairy stories of writers like Geoffrey of Monmouth and Richard of Cirencester, the beginnings of Saxon, or Old English, history are so encumbered with legends, lists of kings, and unidentifiable places that the whole subject is perhaps best left to the theorists. The average reader will find most of these legends and lists merely tedious. The names of Saxon kings like Pantha, Penda, and Pubba tell us little about what was going on in pre-Conquest England, nor does the knowledge that King Ida of Bernicia had twelve sons, one of whom the monk Nennius describes as a 'queen', help us. To add to the confusion, there was a multitude of Celtic 'saints', among them at least three hundred named Colman. Only one or two of these holy men is in any way memorable. Colman of Lindisfarne, who defended the British Easter at the Synod of Whitby; and Colman of Kilmacduagh who trained a cock to awake him for the night-office, a mouse to prevent him from falling asleep afterwards, and a fly to keep his place in his book.

Much more relevant than these odds and ends of information is the question as to who exactly were these Angles, Saxons, and Jutes who changed so completely the course of our history. In view of their importance, we know surprisingly little about them. We know that they came from north-western Germany, first to raid our coasts, then to settle in small bands along the eastern seaboard of what was still Britannia. We can safely say that they were barbarians who could neither read nor write, though they brought with them the ancient sagas of their nation, which were later written down by Christian scribes. But apart from what these epics tell us of their quasi-mythological heroes, the few artefacts that have come down to us reveal little about them except the kind of weapons they used – long spears of iron, round wooden shields, swords, and knives. Excavations of their settlements at West Stow in Suffolk and Mucking in Essex show that their houses were little more than hovels, their agriculture was primitive, their art featureless, their implements and tools crude, and their pottery not much better than the 'mud-pie' type. In brief, they were an Early Iron Age people, far less civilized than their neighbours the Celts and what sophisticated Romans would certainly call savages.

From archaeology we can sketch in only the bare outlines. Literature – one poem in particular – helps fill in the picture. The poem is *Beowulf*, the earliest European vernacular epic and the most significant literary relic of heathen Europe. For it gives us a glimpse of that dark world from whence came the people who were to replace in Britain the language and laws of the Romans. These Teutons are depicted as men of huge stature, always ready to fight, glorying in killing and even being killed, and when not at war, continuously banqueting in vast halls, gorging themselves on meat, and washing down their food with draughts of beer. A warrior in *Beowulf* entertains a lady seated next to him at supper by describing how he had set fire to a city and 'slept in the blood of those who had tried to defend the gates'. *Beowulf* is full of images of violence: 'The foul wretch awaited the mortal wound; a mighty gash was evident upon his shoulder; the sinews sprung asunder, the junctures of the bones burst: victory was given to Beowulf.'[2] The 'foul wretch' was Grendel, a fiend in human shape who periodically dines off those thanes rendered unconscious during a drinking session in Heorot, or Great Hall. Thirty warriors had been devoured when Beowulf appears on the scene and despatches the monster. 'It was a great wonder,' says the bard, 'that the wine-hall fell not down, such was the noise as Beowulf and Grendel hacked away at each other. And after the foul wretch Grendel,

[2] *Beowulf*. Edited . . . by John M. Kemble. London: William Pickering, 1833. p. 32.

came his mother, "the she-wolf of the abyss".' Beowulf takes on this formidable adversary and after letting fly his battle-cry, sets about breaking her neck and finishing her off with 'an old gigantic sword, doughty of age, ready for use. . . . The sword passed through her doomed body. She sank upon the floor. The sword was bloody. The man rejoiced in his deed.'[3]

Such, then, were the people who harried and eventually conquered the whole of what is now England, the Land of the Angles – a people who seem to have been motivated as much by a blood-lust as by the desire for loot, for when they were not slaughtering those they were pillaging, they were fighting among themselves. Out of fourteen Northumbrian kings over a period of a century, seven were slain; six deposed; and only one was allowed to complete his reign.

Yet within four centuries of the coming of these barbarians, a nation, or alliance of nations, had developed which gained the respect of all Europe; and within another millennium their descendants were to rule one third of the globe. What wrought this miraculous change? What spiritual force was able to influence the behaviour of men whose principal occupation up to that time had been brigandage?

The answer in one word is Christianity, even though this was a religion diametrically opposed not only to the ancient Teutonic beliefs, but also to their instincts. Christianity proclaimed the gospel of peace and brotherhood; Wodenism glorified war and genocide. Perhaps even more remarkable was the temerity of the Christian evangelists in getting into the presence of the Saxon chieftains at all in view of the opposition of the pagan priests and the suspicions of the loyal bodyguards. The explanation can only be that the monks who undertook these missions to the tribes were men of outstanding courage. They had the supreme self-confidence which enabled St Germain, bishop of Auxerre, to march up to the Armorican chieftain Goar, seize his horse by the bridle, and give the barbarian a

[3] *op. cit.*, p. 60 *et passim.*

lecture about his bad behaviour. The missionaries had still another advantage. They represented in their manner and bearing something of the *maiestas* of Rome itself. The robed men holding aloft their crosses and chanting their strange liturgies came as emissaries of far greater kings than the tribal leaders – of kings who lived in marble palaces in vast cities, whereas the barbarian chiefs lived in huts in the forests. Neither the God of the Romans nor His ambassadors were to be lightly dismissed.

We can discern the extent to which the Saxons were overawed by the Latin missionaries in the first meeting between St Augustine and the Kentish king Ethelbert in 597. Ethelbert actually believed that the Roman priest was capable of black magic and took care to hold the initial audience in the open air where the visitor's 'spells' would be less effective. But St Augustine had a far better weapon in his armoury than magic: he had the open support of the king's Frankish wife and the tacit sympathy of all the ladies in her entourage. The enormous contribution of women all over the pagan world towards the spread of Christianity cannot be over-emphasized, particularly in countries on the borders of the Roman Empire. Barbarian women may have been permitted to fight side by side with their men in battle, as Caesar noted, but they were not included in councils of state; and they must have been disgusted by the drunken orgies which so often ended in the murder of a husband or son. Theirs was a servile existence, so it is not surprising that they listened sympathetically to the foreigners who promised them a more dignified and rewarding role in society. In nearly every case of the conversion of the Saxon kings, wives and daughters were instrumental in bringing about the royal acceptance of the new religion. Thanks to them, the success of the missionaries, despite the most difficult and dangerous conditions, was remarkable. And in view of the difficulties and dangers, it was no wonder that a timid monk like St Augustine dreaded his assignment to England and *en route* requested Pope Gregory to relieve him of it. He did not speak the language, he complained, knew little or nothing about the people, and in his heart of hearts regarded them as near-savages. When he did arrive, he had to contend with the pagan clergy who were naturally not disposed to surrender their powers and privileges. Fortunately for Augustine, King Ethelbert had married Bertha, the Christian daughter of the Frankish king Charibert, and she, as the cleverer of the two, must have had a strong influence on a man who was overawed by, if not positively afraid of, suave foreigners like the Italian Augustine. Bertha's daughter, Ethelburga, a Christian like her mother, played a vital role in the conversion of heathen England to Christianity. She had been promised in marriage to Edwin, king of Northumbria, provided she was allowed to practise her religion and be accompanied by her own clergy. It was Ethelburga who facilitated the visit of Paulinus, another Italian missionary, to Edwin in AD 626. He came with letters and gifts from Pope Gregory. Bede describes Paulinus as 'a tall man with a slight stoop, black hair, thin face, and a narrow aquiline nose'. He sounds like the archetype of those haughty prelates who became the power behind the thrones of European kings, the *eminences grises* of mediaeval politics. Unlike St Augustine, a timid soul, Paulinus was a man of strong character, for he was actually able to persuade his chief opponent, the heathen high priest Coifi, to renounce his ancient gods and to set fire to Woden's temple at Goodmanham, twenty miles from York. Shortly afterwards, Edwin, too, embraced Christianity. Only one obstacle delayed the king's complete acceptance of the new faith: he was chary of the ritual of baptism which entailed complete submersion in the nearest river. He suspected a trap. For he had recently seized the throne of Northumbria by murdering the lawful king, and he may have had a foreboding that he would be disposed of in his turn, perhaps while he was being baptized. He was, a few years later, killed in battle by his rival, Penda of Mercia, who immediately destroyed the Christian churches and drove Paulinus into exile.

But despite set-backs, Christianity spread steadily throughout the British Isles during the seventh century. East Anglia was converted in 630 by a papal mission led by the French monk, Felix. In 634, Aidan, the Irishman, brought the gospel to Bernicia, the more northern of the two kingdoms of Northumbria. The Italian missionary Berin was less successful. He had been assigned to the Midlands, but had to report back to Rome that the population was so hostile that he could make no progress. However, notwithstanding some resistance by the pagans, almost the whole country had become Christian by the end of the eighth century. National as well as spiritual unity now seemed possible, but unfortunately neither the kings nor the priests could agree on a common policy. The rulers of the various kingdoms continued to jostle for temporal power and the Christian Church split into two rival camps – the Church that had survived since Roman times in Celtic Britain; and the Church introduced from Rome into Anglo-Saxon England. These two institutions were as different from each other as a Welsh hermit perched on a rock in the Bristol Channel from an Italian priest officiating at the court of a king. Such holy men were almost two separate species in their manner of life and worship, and the churches they served were separate organizations. The Celtic Church, cut off from Rome for several centuries, continued to observe the rule of the Romano-British Fathers – SS Illtud, Samson, Patrick, David, and others of West Country origin. It was a Church of fraternities and sororities, of communities who lived independently of a central authority, sometimes in 'double monasteries' where monks and nuns lived together, sometimes in hermitages, and sometimes in bands of wandering priests who, rough in dress and speech, were far from welcome in the polished society of the Roman Catholics. As far as the papal bishops were concerned, these 'intruding clergy', as the Celtic priests were called, were a nuisance: they had no letters of credit from any recognized ecclesiastical authority and they did not accept the rule of chastity. On the contrary, most of them had wives and (it was suspected) mistresses picked up during their wanderings.

But despite the criticism that monks and nuns lived in mixed communities, the British rule was actually more rigorous than the Roman. The successors to the original Italian and French priests who had brought Christianity to Anglo-Saxon England were certainly not ascetics like the monks of Iona who lived a life of severe austerity, but they had introduced some of the elegance and luxury of the Mediterranean world into a land still primitive by the standards of continental Europe. They were already patronizing and harnessing the arts to the service of their Church, building the great monasteries and cathedrals of the new Europe, employing master-masons, glass-makers, and the finest craftsmen in every field, and founding schools where the literature and science of the old classical world were studied. The British clergy, in contrast, clinging to their old beliefs that the things of this world must be totally rejected, had little sympathy with noble architecture, artistic ornamentation, or the pomp and ceremony used by the Catholic prelates to impress ambitious monarchs of petty kingdoms. Moreover, there was now a deeper cause of division between the two churches, a matter of fundamental doctrinal importance: the date of Easter, the oldest and most sacred of the Christian festivals.

To us to-day, this controversy, like so many contentious quarrels of the early Church, may seem trifling, if not outright ridiculous, but it was not so to those bishops and their congregations whose orthodoxy was challenged. The issue as to whether Easter should be observed, as it was by the apostles, on the day the Jews celebrate the Feast of the Passover, or at the time decreed by the Council of Nicaea had divided the Christian world for decades. The problem of fixing this feast arose from a difficulty of computation. The Jewish lunar and the Christian solar calendars could not be made to agree. The Jewish Passover, for instance, always falls on the evening of the fourteenth day of the Jewish month of Nisan, whereas Easter, calculated according to the Roman calendar, had become a movable feast. The Celtic Church, however, continued to observe it on the day of Passover, the Roman Church on the day following the full moon after the vernal equinox.

The importance of all this in eighth-century England was that the Celtic Church was almost the last communion to defy Rome and in so doing to isolate itself from the rest of Christendom. But the British and Irish bishops were not prepared to give up their ancient beliefs at the behest of foreigners; and so deep-seated was their suspicion of the Roman priests that fraternization between the two churches was to all intents and purposes non-existent. Their leaders even quarrelled about the correct shape of the tonsure, although it was the paschal problem which was to cause the greatest acrimony and confusion. And since the kings of the different regions naturally supported the bishops they had themselves appointed, the controversy was liable to aggravate territorial and political disputes between Kent, East Anglia, and Wessex, kingdoms which belonged to the Roman faction, and Northumbria and Mercia which were loyal to the old Church. The unsatisfactory state of affairs was exemplified by the crisis at the court of King Oswy of Northumbria. Oswy had been baptized and brought up by monks of the Celtic Church and consequently celebrated Easter according to their usage. His wife, on the other hand, had been educated by a Roman chaplain and held to the Roman method of computing the feast. As a result, the king and his court might be celebrating the Resurrection with joy and feasting while in the very same place his queen and the holy men and women of her party were still fasting on Good Friday. Not surprisingly the unseemliness of the situation caused considerable embarrassment, and such was the dissension throughout the land, especially between the north and south, that King Oswy was obliged to convoke a conference of the leaders of the two churches to give them an opportunity to prove who was right and so settle the matter once and for all. This most important synod which was to determine the future role of the Church in Britain was held in AD 664 at a monastery in the Northumbrian town of Whitby, with King Oswy presiding.

The principal actors who played out the drama of the Synod of Whitby are all fascinating characters of early English history, even though their names and deeds and words are scarcely remembered. King Oswy was a typical Saxon chieftain who had come to supreme power in the kingdom of Northumbria by war and, where it was expedient, by the cold-blooded murder of his rivals. Such men, though they could hardly be reckoned devout Christians, were nearly always deferential to their priests and continually sought ways and means of gaining their approval. As atonement for the murder of his kinsman Oswin, for example, Oswy donated a large tract of land to the Church for the erection of a monastery. And before beginning his war against the Mercians, he vowed in return for victory to give his little daughter as a virgin to God as well as twelve estates to the Church for the foundation of twelve more monasteries. And when he grew old and feeble, he begged Bishop Wilfrid to accompany him to Rome so that the pope himself could give him absolution. There is no doubt that such an old-fashioned Saxon chief conceived heaven as a bigger and better mead hall where non-stop revels like those described in *Beowulf* took place.

This was the president of the synod who was to pronounce judgment and so decide for all time when Easter was to be celebrated. Chief spokesman for the Celtic party was the Irish bishop, Colman, abbot of Lindisfarne, supported by a large following of Irish monks described by the Catholic delegation as 'intractable men of a harsh and barbarous dispostion'. This supercilious dismissal of his followers could not, however, detract from the veneration in which Bishop Colman was held, for he had started his vocation as a pupil of the great missionary bishop of Northumbria, Aidan, in the monastery of Iona, following in the footsteps of the Celtic saints by living an austere and continent life, devoting all his time and energy to preaching and good works, and having neither home, possessions, nor even any money. His example had had a tremendous effect on both the ordinary folk and the nobles, many of whom abandoned their pagan ways and retired to monasteries in the hope of attaining the heaven of the Christians.

The champion of the Romans at the Synod was a marked contrast. Wilfrid, bishop of York, was in his way representative of a new generation of prelates who were to dominate ecclesiastical and civil politics over the next thousand years. A protégé of Queen Eanfled, King Oswy's wife, he was sent to Lindisfarne to be educated and then encouraged to set out on a pilgrimage to Rome. After several years of continental travel, he returned to his native land, to be welcomed at the court of the English kings, one of whom, Alfrith of Deira, gave him a monastery at Ripon, first turning out the resident monks who belonged to the Celtic Church. Wilfrid immediately introduced the Rule of St Benedict into the monastery and instituted the Roman method of calculating Easter. A handsome, aristocratic, and sophisticated priest, he was the obvious choice for challenging the old leaders of the Celtic Church like the legendary St Columba, the universally venerated Aidan, and the much loved Colman.

The last of these holy men began his defence by referring to John the Apostle's celebration of Easter on the fourteenth day of the Jewish month of Nisan, stating that what was good enough for a disciple of Jesus was good enough for a simple monk like him. It had been good enough, too, for St Columba. Colman's supporters loudly applauded what must have seemed an unanswerable argument. But they had underestimated Wilfrid's intellectual subtlety. This ecclesiastic who had been tutored by some of the most learned prelates of Europe answered Colman's argument by pointing out that it was St Peter, the Holder of the Keys, who must be obeyed in these matters and that it was folly for a small group inhabiting the outermost islands on the fringe of the Ocean to challenge the chosen apostle's authority which had been inherited by the Roman Catholic Church. Those who had the temerity to do so, he added, had often been denounced as heretics at many previous synods. 'You don't want to be thought a heretic, do you?' inquired Wilfrid, *with a smile*, as the record says. Colman no doubt noted that smile, coupled with the dreaded word 'heretic', and he launched into a somewhat confused defence of his position by referring to St Columba whose sanctity, he pointed out, was recognized not only by his fellow-Irishmen, but by his English horse. Wilfrid was not much impressed, and replied haughtily that Colman, as an Irishman, placed too much value on horse sense. Columba, he said, though no doubt a holy man, was also something of a rustic, and the fact that he had a voice audible a mile away was not justification for setting him against Peter, Prince of the Apostles.

Wilfrid won the day. King Oswy, perhaps influenced by his wife, perhaps realizing that the day of the hermit-monks was over, found for the Romans. Colman and his monks showed their displeasure by abandoning their monastery on Lindisfarne and returning to Iona, taking the bones of St Aidan with them. They could never admit that such a holy man, much less St Columba, had been capable of error. About thirty English monks also decided to go with them, the whole group eventually crossing to Ireland to found still another monastery on the island of Inishbofin in County Galway. Alas! This was not a happy venture, for relations between the Irish and English were already strained by the habit of the Irish monks of leaving the monastery to go a-wandering during the pleasant months of summer, abandoning their English brothers to gather in the harvest. When this was done and food was abundant again, the Irish re-appeared, demanding an equal share of the available victuals and more than their share of the home-brew. We are told that eventually the inmates actually came to blows at Inishbofin and shortly after the monastery was abandoned.

The Synod of Whitby in 664 was, in its way, as important a milestone in British history as the Act of Union of 1801. It symbolized the end of the old British Church. The whole of England had adopted the Roman Easter by AD 670. Ireland followed suit in 692; northern Scotland in 710; the monks of Iona in 716; and last, Wales in 768. From now on there were to be no officially approved hermits, wandering bishops, 'intruding clergy', or mixed communities of monks and nuns. It became harder, too, to become a saint. In the time of SS Patrick and David there had been literally hundreds of British saints. And even though the Roman Church was sceptical of this plenitude of holy men and women, it wisely took no steps to belittle the Gwens, Nons, Guwals, Petrocs, and a host of other local patrons. Their cults lingered on throughout the Middle Ages in the remoter parishes of England and Wales until Henry VIII systematically destroyed their shrines, looted their churches, and proscribed their cults altogether. Cromwell and his soldiers completed the process of destruction, pulling down statues, smashing stained glass windows, vandalizing church murals, and destroying illuminated manuscripts. The names of those early British saints which do survive are found, with few exceptions, in the West Country where a village is sometimes called after them, like St Erth, St Ewe, and St Teach in Cornwall.

What is perhaps most significant about these obscure and now mostly forgotten British saints is that they were canonized by popular acclaim, not by papal decree. Nobody after Pope Innocent III (1199–1216) was sanctified unless his life and alleged miracles had been thoroughly investigated, and under this new dispensation a candidate had to have achieved more than the miracle of turning bath water into beer, as in the case of the Irish nun St Brigid, to be eligible for canonization. Beatification being no longer a national prerogative, many British proto-martyrs, including Charles I, have never been officially sanctified, although five churches in Britain are dedicated to this monarch's memory, and until Queen Victoria suppressed it, the thirtieth of January was celebrated as his feast day. Yet the custom of sanctifying holy men on the spot, as it were, died hard and the people continued to take it in their own hands to commemorate a local benefactor in this fashion.

Sir John Shorne of Monks Risborough was such an elect. His cult, based, it is said, on his success in catching the devil and imprisoning him in his boot, flourished widely from the fourteenth century and is featured on rood screens in Cawston, Gately, and Suffield in Norfolk. His miraculous powers in curing gout, ague, and toothache are well attested, and his sanctity is revealed in paintings showing how his knees had developed large horny pads from constant kneeling. There is no doubt that in the Celtic Church of pre-Augustine days Sir John's achievements would have qualified him to belong to the company of SS Docco, Veep, Blazey, Rumon, Webb, Day, and the sixty-three children of St Brychan.

The Anglo-Saxon period from AD 450 to 900 (death of King Alfred) is so varied and in many respects so obscure that it is difficult even to differentiate between the three separate peoples – Angles, Saxons, and Jutes – and the many kingdoms which rose and fell before this land became one nation. But one event stands out as the most significant happening of these times: the conversion of several backward heathen tribes into one civilized Christian nation whose literature and art were to become superior to anything produced in northern Europe. All this took place within a hundred years, from the germinal date of 596, when St Augustine arrived, to 686 when the entire country had been converted. The speed of the change-over from the crude concepts of Wodenism to the Christian faith has not been fully appreciated or adequately explained, especially the crucial role that women played in this drama. We must add to that factor the apparent ease with which the first foreign missionaries travelled about a lawless country, crossed frontiers from one feuding kingdom to another, and gained authority over chieftains whose language they could not even speak. We are not told how they accomplished these feats, but the results were spectacular. A barbarian people who could not read or write when they landed on these shores in the fifth century were actually to become conversant in the Greek and Latin languages several generations later; a people who could only build primitive shelters of daub and wattle were erecting cathedrals of stone; and tribal bards who once eulogized the art of mayhem in the mead-hall of some blood-thirsty chieftain had been metamorphosized into gentle poets of the monasteries.

Yet it is difficult to believe – since we have no firm evidence for or against – that the common people were much affected by this enormous spiritual and intellectual advance; and one could go farther and ask if the Saxon kings and nobles themselves were basically changed in their behaviour by the sermons and lectures they submitted to out of respect for the foreign priests. A characteristic example of a royal convert was the Bernician king, Oswy, who, as we have noted, conceived of the Christian heaven as a Northumbrian palace where the traditional Saxon feasting went on as usual. Other kings and princes relapsed into paganism, and in some cases chased their priestly councillors out of their kingdoms. The aristocrat Paulinus, bishop of York, was such a casualty when King Edwin of Northumbria whom he had converted was killed and ousted by the Mercian King Penda, a pagan, at the Battle of Hatfield Chase in 633. Paulinus had to flee Northumbria together with those Christians noble or rich enough to escape the roving bands of looters who spared neither sex nor age. Yet it is not strictly accurate to say that large areas of England had actually *relapsed*, since it is unlikely that the slaves and serfs owned by the clergy as well as the nobility were ever other than lukewarm Christians.

The struggle between paganism and Christianity continued for much longer in England than the Church historians admit, and it was aggravated in a very particular respect by the innate hostility between the Celtic and Roman churchmen. None the less, religion was the determining factor in the creation of England and, more than that, of an English king like Alfred, at once soldier, sailor, legislator, architect, master-craftsman, author, and scholar. It was the Christian teaching which enabled this Saxon nobleman to develop his genius, for whereas he would have been able neither to read nor write as a heathen princeling, as the son of pious Christian parents he was given the education of a Roman aristocrat. The result was our first and greatest king of England.

CANTERBURY (Kent): the Cradle of British Christianity

Guidebook: Boyle, John. *Canterbury Pilgrim's Guide*. Illustrations and plans. Canterbury: the Corporation, 1976.

The story of English Christianity begins not at the Cathedral of Canterbury, but at St Martin's, 'the Mother Church of England'. St Martin's claim to be the oldest church in Europe in which Christian worship has been offered without a break seems plausible. Bede, writing in 731 when parts of the Roman city of Durovernum were still standing, describes the church as being of Roman origin. This suggests that the Christian edifice had been converted from a pagan temple. The church was certainly there in 562 when the princess Bertha, daughter of King Charibert of Paris, arrived in Canterbury as the bride of King Ethelbert, for at one time St Martin's was thought to be her burial place, although excavations of the south-east porticus of SS Peter and Paul revealed her tomb to be alongside that of her husband. The first eight archbishops of Canterbury, including St Augustine himself, are entombed across the nave in the same church. They are: St Augustine (601–04), the 'Apostle of the English'; St Laurentius (605–19) who claimed he was beaten black and blue by St Peter for cowardice and then frightened Ethelbert's son Edbald into becoming a Christian by showing him his scarred back; St Mellitus (619–24) a Roman abbot of noble birth, who greatly suffered from gout and saved a church from being burnt by standing in the path of the flames; St Justus (624–27), the first bishop of London who refused to administer the sacrament to the pagan sons of King Edbald; St Honorius (627–53), one of the second contingent of Roman monks sent to England by Pope Gregory to convert the heathen (he sent missionaries to the last outposts of the Saxon pagans); St Deusdedit (653–64), the first Anglo-Saxon, whose English name was Frithona, to occupy the see; St Theodore (666–90), a Greek monk who replaced an African abbot as the pope's choice for the archbishopric following the death of Deusdedit. He was the most scholarly and most important of the archbishops between Augustine and the Norman, Lanfranc. In a sense he was the founder of the Church of England in his work of fusing the different elements of the Roman, British, and Irish sects. Three years after St Theodore came St Berhtwald (693–731), a Saxon monk 'by no means to be compared in learning with his predecessor', according to Bede.

Canterbury Cathedral, although begun by St Augustine as part of his extensive church building programme, has nothing Saxon or Roman about it, for the original shrine was burnt down by the Danes in 1011 when its archbishop, Alphege, was murdered. The present cathedral is early Norman and is mostly the work of the master-mason William the Frenchman (1176–8) and his successor William the Englishman (1178–80). Its mediaeval history, like its architecture, takes us a long way from the simplicity of the time of Ethelbert, Bertha, and Augustine through a succession of grim and tragic happenings, beginning with the murder of Thomas à Becket in 1170, the brutal beheading of Simon of Sudbury by Wat Tyler and his rabble in 1381, the burning at the stake of Cranmer in 1556, and the execution of Laud in 1645. Henry VIII even made an attempt to degrade the great shrine by burning the ashes of Becket and scattering them to the wind before looting the saint's tomb of 312 lb of gold; but neither he nor any other tyrant could detract from the majesty of a cathedral which sanctifies the birthplace of English Christianity.

The shrine of St Thomas in the Trinity Chapel is now the holiest place in the cathedral since it became the goal of the Canterbury pilgrims, 100,000 of whom used to visit the martyr's tomb every year before Henry VIII desecrated it. Immediately after Becket's canonization, miracles were said to be worked at his grave in the crypt and even at the well in which his garments had been washed. His *cultus*, in fact, was responsible for the growth and prosperity of Canterbury even more than the city's associations with St Augustine, and as the number of hostels for the accommodation of visitors increased, the pilgrimage became not only a pious exercise, but a favourite place for summer excursions. Chaucer's account of such an expedition, with pilgrims of all classes and types leisurely enjoying the journey and telling stories along the road, sums up what Canterbury meant throughout the Middle Ages.

Chaucer, the pilgrims, and Thomas à Becket are still very much present in spirit even to the tourist arriving by motor-coach, but Augustine, Ethelbert, and Bertha are not. The Normans systematically erased the monuments of the Saxon kings and their archbishops, even demolishing the monastery of Christ Church and the great octagonal rotunda of Wulfric, abbot of St Augustine's in the eleventh century. Consequently the searcher for relics will find only broken walls to show where the first saints and the first Christian kings worshipped.

SUTTON HOO (Suffolk): the Last of the Pagan Tombs

Guidebook: *The Sutton Hoo Ship Burial. A Handbook.* London: British Museum, 1978.

Sutton Hoo is the name of a private estate across the River Deben from the town of Woodbridge in south-east Suffolk. The nearest large town is Ipswich. Sutton Hoo was the site of an oval mound, or 'ship-barrow', originally 12′ high and over 100′ long. This barrow when excavated in 1939 was found to be the tomb of a king or great chieftain buried with his warship. The ship, of which only the impression imprinted in the earth remains, was seen to be a clinker-built vessel 90′ long with a beam of 14½′, constructed to be propelled by 38 oarsmen, 19 a side. The cabin of this ship yielded a hoard of grave goods so

22 The bronze stag surmounted the sceptre of the East Anglian king Raedwald whose warship, but not his body, was entombed at Sutton Hoo. Excavations of the burial mount yielded the richest haul of Anglo-Saxon treasures in the annals of archaeology.

23 An old photograph shows the excavation of the Sutton Hoo warship.

rich that Sutton Hoo has been pronounced the most splendid archaeological discovery ever made in the British Isles. But there was a mystery connected with the tomb: it contained no body, and never had done so.

The artefacts found in this royal grave are on permanent exhibition in the British Museum. They can be classified into three categories: 1) arms and armour; 2) ceremonial objects; and 3) household articles, including the utensils required for feasting and entertainment in the great hall of a Saxon chieftain.

All the evidence of this ship-burial points to the traditional interment of a pagan king. The presence of various Christian objects like the silver spoons inscribed in Greek *Saulos* and *Paulos* does not alter that fact, for Christians took nothing with them to the grave. Pagans took everything they thought might be needed in the after-life.

The hundreds of burial mounds found all over Suffolk were looted long ago, with one or two exceptions; but all would have contained grave goods as varied and valuable as befitted the status of the deceased. The unknown chieftain of Sutton Hoo was provided with a large assortment of weapons, his battle standard, his sceptre, a suit of golden armour, and everything required for continuing his royal pursuits in the next world, even a harp and seven huge drinking horns.

Then who was he? And why is there no body in the tomb?

What evidence we have points to one man only – Raedwald, king of the East Angles. Raedwald was a warrior-king who died in 624. In his life and beliefs, he was typical of seventh-century England and its kings, even to claiming to be tenth in descent from Woden, the German god of battles. He was typical in his ambivalence about religion, for in common with many other chieftains of his time, he decided that the Christian God and the Christian faith, backed by the majesty of Rome and the Church, were the best guarantees for earthly success. Raedwald had seen how his neighbour, King Ethelbert of Kent, had flourished after the arrival of the Roman missionaries led by

Augustine, and on a visit to Canterbury was persuaded to recognize the new God and actually allowed himself to be baptized, which in the seventh century meant complete immersion. But on his return to his capital at Rendlesham, to-day a hamlet four miles north-east of Woodbridge, his wife, undoubtedly influenced by the priests, persuaded him to stay true to his ancestral religion. To be both Christian and pagan at one and the same time may have caused problems for some men, monarchs among them; but Raedwald easily resolved his dilemma by building a temple in which there were two altars served by two bodies of priests – one for Christian sacrifice, the other for sacrifice to heathen idols. It seems that this simple pantheism worked very well, and it also explains why Raedwald's body is not found in the ship at Sutton Hoo. He was taking no chances with his after-life. His body was probably buried in a Christian tomb, in a church or monastery where all Christian kings were laid to rest; his spirit was allowed to join his pagan forefathers in the old German tradition. So whichever god was supreme, and whichever religion was the true faith, Raedwald felt that he had taken every precaution to secure for himself a safe hereafter.

The manner of commemorating him was traditional. In the old days, a warship was either interred with a great warrior or sent in flames out to sea. The ship was the symbol of his battles on land and sea. The grave goods were symbolic – battle-standard, sceptre, royal insignia, arms and armour, vessels for feasting, instruments for entertainment, a treasury of gold and silver. To be able to afford a burial on the scale of Sutton Hoo, a monarch had to be immensely rich as well as powerful. There was no king in seventh-century England who met these requirements, except Raedwald, at the time ruler over most of the eastern English provinces south of the Humber.

But we still do not know where he was actually buried, perhaps in the 'temple' he built to accommodate the Christian as well as the heathen god. This wooden building would have been located near the royal residence at Rendlesham, four miles to the north of the Sutton Hoo burial ground on the same river, the Deben. Nothing has ever been found of this palace which Bede specifically mentions as being located at Rendlesham, but that is understandable. A Saxon hall before the continental masons arrived consisted of a large timber construction like a mediaeval barn, its walls decorated with tapestries, shields, and weapons. It would easily have burnt or been torn down, leaving no ruins to show where it stood, and the archaeologists have found none despite intensive searching.

Once the burial mound at Sutton Hoo had been excavated and photographed, the site was covered over, and there is now nothing to see of the actual barrow. But the Suffolk landscape along the banks of the Deben has changed little from Saxon times when this reach of the river was a royal cemetery. There are still sixteen barrows of varying heights in the vicinity, with many graves in between. A walk around the site should be followed by a visit to the magnificent exhibition of grave goods in the British Museum.

WHITBY (Yorkshire): the Abbess and the Poet

Guidebook: *Whitby, Yorkshire.* Official guide. Whitby: Horne & Son, 1980.

Whitby, in North Yorkshire at the mouth of the River Esk, incorporates every period of English history, from the coming of the Saxon invaders around AD 550 to the arrival of the bingo halls of recent decades, but it is especially important as a spiritual and intellectual centre of Anglo-Saxon England, a place which helped to shape the national culture for the next thousand years. Yet reminders of the saintly abbess Hilda, of King Oswy, ruler of Northumbria, of our first truly English poet, Caedmon, are few and far between, and the visitor will have to go up to the ruins of the Abbey, perched above the old town on the east side of the harbour, to glimpse something of the original *Streoneshalch*, which Bede translates as *Sinus Phari* or *Lighthouse Bay*. Here was the site of the double monastery of St Hilda, the first abbess. The life of this pious lady who was related to the kings of Northumbria and East Anglia tells us a great deal about the status of women in seventh-century England. To begin with, it is clear that there was enough equality between the sexes for Hilda to be elected the director of what was a leading political as well as religious institution. According to Bede, kings and prelates came to her for advice. Her job as abbess of a double monastery which housed both monks and nuns under the same roof was not easy; but she seems to have been a very efficient organizer and a skilful politician who extended her influence far beyond the walls of her abbey, which she persuaded King Oswy to choose as the conference centre for the Synod of Whitby. Under her rule Whitby became a centre of learning and piety renowned throughout Europe for two hundred years, until the Danes destroyed it completely, laid waste the town that had grown up around it, and massacred the inhabitants.

The ruins of the Abbey one sees to-day are not those of St Hilda but of the Norman soldier-monk Reinfrid who rebuilt the monastery at his own expense in 1078, so we see nothing of the buildings where King Oswy presided over the Synod of Whitby. The Abbess Hilda was, of course, present at this Synod as manageress of the proceedings, as were Colman, Bishop of Lindisfarne, Eanfled, the queen of Northumbria, James the Deacon, Agilbert the Frank, Bishop of Dorchester, and hundreds of monks and itinerant priests. Here, too, somewhere beneath the Norman abbey was the cell of Caedmon who, while sitting in the cow-byre, received the command from a heavenly visitor to sing 'the going forth out of Egypt, the suffering and resurrection of the Lord'. It was the abbess Hilda who encouraged him to versify *The Story of the Fall* which strays a little from orthodoxy in sympathizing with Adam and Eve and questioning a God who allowed his own children to be so cruelly deceived. But the herdsman's bewilderment was in no way

24 The ruins of the abbey of Whitby, built in 1078 on the site of the double monastery of St Hilda. This holy place was the venue of the Synod of Whitby presided over by King Oswy of Northumbria in AD 664. The cell of Caedmon, the first English poet, is said to lie beneath the crypt of the ruined abbey.

cynical, for Bede writes of him that 'no trivial or vain song came from his lips, for he learnt the art of poetry not from man but from God.'

The other poet associated with the Abbey was Godric the Hermit (1069–1170), pedlar, merchant, shipmaster, pirate, and pilgrim who settled down late in life in a well-found cave where he entertained with equal courtesy men and beasts. Frozen birds and rabbits found on the moors were welcome to share his fire. The hunted stag also found protection in his hermitage, and the hunters demanding its ejection from the cave were told that he was not willing to betray a guest.

The succession of pious and learned men and women who made Whitby as famous in Saxon England as Canterbury or York ended with the final destruction of their abbey and monastery by Henry VIII and his adviser, Thomas Cromwell. A new era began for Whitby which reached its zenith in the nineteenth century as a busy commercial harbour and the foremost whaling port of Europe.

What survives of the 'old town' now speaks to us more of the greatest of English navigators, James Cook, than of the first English poet, Caedmon, or of St Hilda, abbess, who 'never failed to serve God when in health and to remain grateful to him even in adversity'.

[7]

OUT OF THE DARKNESS

Grant me, O Son of the Living God,
A little hut in the wilderness to be my dwelling,
A merry lark to nest nearby,
A clear pool to wash away my sins,
A wood to enclose my home,
And the song of birds. . . .

The Hermit's Song. Irish poem (c.850)

One summer morning in the year 699, Guthlac, a monk of the double monastery housing both monks and nuns at Repton, Derbyshire, set out to find himself a hermitage as far away from all human contact as possible. It was his hope to follow in the footsteps of those athletes of Christ who had renounced the world. *Saint* Guthlac, as he was to become, was the son of a Saxon noble and friend of Ethelbald, destined to be king of the East Anglians. The life and times of these two men run parallel: both are representative of what the old historians called the Dark Age, the age of almost continuous wars, of violence, and lawlessness, and, at the same time, of virtue and self-abnegation. The very term, Dark Age, invokes a world in which a hermit was the friend of a king who included among his impieties the violation of nuns in their own convents. Yet Guthlac blesses Ethelbald, Ethelbald honours Guthlac.

If we want a true picture of what life was like in Dark Age England, we will find it much more vividly presented in the history of St Guthlac by the monk Felix than in the monuments on display in our musuems. For Guthlac was a child of his age. Brought up in his father's 'hall', the roughly built edifice of wood and thatch of a Saxon chief, he was nurtured on the old

German sagas endlessly praising the mighty deeds of the tribal heroes. It is hardly surprising that, wanting to emulate them, he formed a band of like-minded young companions and went about the countryside killing, looting and burning. Such was the normal, indeed practically the only career open to a young Anglo-Saxon nobleman in the seventh century.

But in Guthlac's case there occurred a crisis of conscience:

> He thought upon the deaths at the end of dissolute lives of his ancestral line of ancient kings and considered on his nightly ponderings the glories of this earthly life and drew back in horror from the thought of his own inevitable end.[1]

It seems a curious way for a young man of twenty-four surrounded by his fellow-roisterers to think about the future, especially as the band had amassed immense booty in their raids on villages and farms. Perhaps a better clue to the mystery of Guthlac's conversion is the likelihood that the law, such as it was, had caught up with him. At all events, he now disappears into a double monastery presided over by the abbess Elfthryth. Was this neutral territory perhaps the only safe place for him to hide?

It seems that he was not popular in the monastery on account of his refusing all intoxicating liquors and other pleasant drinks, including fruit juice. This question of what and how much a monk could drink was always a sensitive one, especially as some of the brothers were reputed to over-indulge. There were reports of them falling about in the cloisters and even of tumbling down the wells on their way back from vigils. But there was never any official proscription about drinking, and great was the resentment if the abbot attempted to interfere with the victuals. The very last abbot of the monastery dedicated to St Guthlac, John Wells of Crowland, was criticized in

[1] *Felix's Life of St Guthlac.* Introduction, Text, and Notes by Bertram Colgrave. Cambridge: U. P., 1956. p. 83.

1511 for 'cheating the monks of their soup, wine, and pudding.'[2]

It was possibly Guthlac's excessive abstemiousness which eventually decided him to leave the monastery and subject himself to the ordeal of complete isolation in the Anglian marshes, at the time one of the loneliest and most forbidding regions in England – 'the dismal fen of immense size, consisting now of marshes, now of bogs, sometimes of black waters overhung by fog, sometimes studded with wooded islands and traversed by the windings of tortuous streams'.[3] The name of this place was Crowland, to-day a village of 3000 people in one of the most intensively farmed districts of England.

Guthlac had to be rowed across to the island in a fisherman's skiff, his guide having first warned him that no man had ever managed to survive in such a wilderness – 'apparently because of the vagaries of the infesting demons'. The assailants were no little buzzing mosquitoes, or even big growling wolves, but 'redoubtable bands of unearthly spirits' who penetrated the hermit's cell by every crack and cranny.

> They were savage in appearance, terrifying in shape, with great hands, long necks, lean visage, sallow skins, unkempt beards, bristly ears, forbidding brow, savage eyes, fetid breath, horse teeth, flame-vomiting gullets, inflamed throats, thick lips, raucous voices, dirt-encrusted hair, swollen cheeks, bulging chests, scabrous thighs, knock-knees, bowlegs, protuberant ankles, and splay feet.[4]

Despite these aberrations of a mind obviously on the verge of madness, Guthlac stayed on the island and made his home in a mound of clods, eventually building himself a little hut. He abandoned his monkish garb and clothed himself in the skins of beasts. His daily ration of food was a piece of bread eaten only

[2] *The Victoria History of the County of Lincoln*. London: James Street, 1906. Vol. ii, p. 117.

[3] *Felix's Life*, p. 87.

[4] *op. cit.*, p. 103.

after sunset and washed down with 'contaminated water' from the creek. It is hardly surprising that he was soon being visited by 'redoubtable bands of unearthly spirits'. Perhaps some of these long-necked, unkempt, foul-mouthed, and bow-legged visitors were real people, robbers who roamed the countryside, or local fishermen. The former seem on occasion to have thrown him into 'the scummy swamp'. The latter must have brought him his sparse rations. His only companions now were the birds who perched on his head and shoulders; and perhaps nothing illustrates that tenderness felt for wild creatures by the Saxons than the description of the hermit helping to arrange a nesting-place for the swallows who came back to the hermitage year after year and 'asked advice for building their home'.

So Guthlac's story really does sum up the age in which he lived, for the combination of violence and quietism which characterized his behaviour is paralleled in the life of almost every leader, whether king or hermit. It is this that makes his friendship with the exiled nobleman Ethelbald so significant, for this was the future king who one moment was robbing churches and using violence against nuns and the next was living as a disciple at Guthlac's hermitage. It was this same Ethelbald who was so committed to religion that he founded the monastery dedicated to St Guthlac at Crowland[5] and yet so bloodthirsty that he was eventually murdered by his own guards.

No one who studies that Dark Age can ignore the paradoxes of a world in which a king like Ethelbald was on one of the English thrones, a hermit like Guthlac was holding court in a watery wilderness, and a monk like Bede was familiar with all the knowledge preserved from the ancient world. Such incredible contrasts were reflected in the landscape itself, for the countryside was well cultivated and prosperous in places, wild and dangerous in others, uninhabitable in still others. The

[5] Some historians dispute this tradition which, they maintain, was invented by fourteenth-century forgers.

tribes were continually at war, and most of the population was involved, largely against their will, in fighting. England was not yet a nation, and the innumerable Anglo-Saxon chieftains, many of them with barbarous and near-unpronounceable names, move across the stage of history in shadowy procession and then disappear into a limbo of myth and legend. There were, in fact, hundreds of them. Between AD 455 and 1066, there were 26 kings of Kent; 7 kings of Deira; 35 kings of Bernicia; 28 kings of Northumbria; 21 kings of Mercia; several kings of Lindsey; 15 kings of East Anglia; 56 kings of the Saxons; 2 kings of the Danish kingdom of York; and 12 who claimed to be kings of the entire island – a total of some 223 kings in 600 years. To this total must be added 50 known kings for the Welsh kingdom and an unknown number for Scotland whose monarchy began with King Fergus who came from Ireland about 330 BC. In short, there were so many kings that even the greatest and most powerful of them, Athelstan and Offa and Edmund, seem to be as unreal as the legendary Gog and Magog.

But there is one noteworthy exception: Alfred the Great, King of the English; and though more than 1000 years have passed since his death, his spirit still pervades our history. He is not only our first national king, he alone of his era is a real person. We willingly respond to the story of the burning of cakes, even though the academics dismiss this incident as apocryphal. Kings are not supposed to be sitting in a peasant's hut, ordered to oversee the baking. But Alfred undoubtedly did eat and sleep in such humble homes, and the woman's scolding has the ring of truth to it: 'Ah, how like a man! Couldn't you have turned the cakes over when you saw them burning? Or were you too lazy?'[6] Indeed, the legend helps explain why Alfred is remembered long after we have closed our history books.

[6] L. C. Jane, *Asser's Life of King Alfred*. London: Chatto & Windus, 1926. p. 22.

25 King Alfred, the first 'king of the English' and our only monarch to be called 'The Great', stands overlooking the market square at Wantage, Oxfordshire, where he was said to have been born in AD 849.

Alfred has been called 'The Great' and 'The Truth-Teller'. A cult has grown up around him comparable with that which surrounds the far more shadowy figure of Arthur, 'the last of the Romans'. The reason is that he created the land we know as England, a land in which all the citizens, irrespective of their local loyalties, were to become united in allegiance to a single monarch and a common heritage. Alfred was never king of *all* the English, since a great many of his fellow-countrymen were still subjugated by the Danes who had their own kings and courts. But his biographer, the Welsh Bishop Asser, called him 'ruler of all the Christians of Britain, king of the Angles and Saxons'. In other words, by 886 after years of war, the Danish invaders were driven from most of southern England, a period of comparative peace was possible, and a nation as opposed to a conglomeration of tribes began to emerge. The Dark Age was about to end. It was now that Alfred proved his greatness, now that he laid down the foundations of a national character.

His first concern was neither political nor economic. It was moral: to raise the intellectual standard of the people. He wrote in the preface to his translation of Pope Gregory's *Regula Pastoralis*:

> Formerly men came from overseas, seeking wisdom in our own land; now, if we are to have scholarship at all, we must look for it abroad. So great has been the decay of learning among Englishmen that there are very few anywhere in the country who can understand the Mass or translate a letter from Latin into English. In fact, I cannot remember meeting one such, south of the Thames, when I came to the throne.[7]

As a young Saxon prince, Alfred had been as ignorant as his subjects, but he spent every spare minute he had from the time

[7] *King Alfred's West-Saxon Version of Gregory's Pastoral Care*. London: Early English Text Society. Nos 45, 50. p. 8.

he was a boy in endeavouring to educate himself. To a man who for over twenty years was on the run, pursuing or being pursued by his enemies, the task of learning Latin and of reading the difficult prose of a philosopher like Boethius and then of translating the *Consolation* into a primitive dialect like West Saxon was nothing short of heroic. Scholars brought from many places to help him had to explain the Latin text to him passage by passage. But he was determined to set an example to his nobles and peasants alike, insisting that even a man who was too old to learn to read and so to educate himself, could still be read to by his sons.

But why should a king who had spent most of his life in the company of soldiers be concerned with philosophy and literature? He saw how his nation had relapsed into near-barbarism not only because of the continual wars, but because of ignorance. Many of the monasteries which were the fountain-heads of learning and enlightenment had been destroyed, including Lindisfarne and Jarrow, the home of Bede. Others had neither the money nor resources to feed their inmates. The old ideals of the Celtic saints and Roman missionaries were almost extinguished. It was a Dark Age brought about by a new race of heathens, the Norsemen, romanticized under the title of Vikings and endorsed as genuine contributors to civilization. We are told of their achievements as shipwrights, mariners, navigators, explorers, and traders, and it is true that their 'empire' in terms of seafaring extended from the Arctic to the Mediterranean. But in their own day, no matter where they went, they were regarded as pirates who lived by murder and looting, landing wherever the wind took them, deliberately to destroy and pillage. Their contribution to civilized life in terms of art, literature, and learning was negligible compared with the devastation they caused. This, at any rate, was the view recorded in *The Anglo-Saxon Chronicle* in the earliest reference to their coming to these shores: 'An DCC XCIII [793] On the sixth of the Ides of January [Jan 8], the havoc of heathen men [i.e. the Norsemen] miserably destroyed God's church at Lindisfarne through rapine and slaughter.'[8] And 216 years later they were still at it, as the entry in the *Chronicle* for the year 1010 shows:

> For three months they harried and burned, ay even into the wild fens [of East Anglia] they went, and there slew men and cattle and burned throughout the fens. And Thetford they burned and Cambridge. And afterwards they went south to the Thames . . . and ever burned as they went. . . . Then before St Andrew's mass-day [Nov 30], they came to Northampton and speedily burned that town, and thence went over the Thames into Wessex and burned all that.[9]

They finished off this grand tour of burning and looting by abducting the archbishop of Canterbury and a number of abbots and abbesses, murdering the archbishop by 'pelting him with bones and with the heads of oxen until one of them struck him on the head with an axe, so that he sank down and his holy blood fell on the earth.'[10]

A brief respite for the people of southern England from a hundred years of this kind of rapine came only after Alfred had finally trapped and defeated the Danish army at Edington in Wiltshire in 878. Here he won a decisive victory. The Danes surrendered and their king, Guthrum, agreed to become a Christian. He was baptized with thirty of his chiefs in the presence of Alfred at Athelney in Somerset. The two kings then went together to the royal villa at Wedmore and signed a peace treaty. The Danes agreed to leave most of southern England to Alfred; and this concession gave him those fourteen years of peace within which to implement his plan for laying the foundations of a new nation.

One of his first tasks was to establish schools for the sons of

[8] *The Anglo-Saxon Chronicle.* Edited with a translation by Benjamin Thorpe. London: Longman, Green, 1861. Vol. ii, p. 48.

[9] *op. cit.*, p. 116.

[10] Jane, *op. cit.*, p. 117.

nobles and those boys of humbler birth who were apt students. The essence of the curriculum was the study of the Latin and Saxon languages and, if possible, of Greek, for the Anglo-Saxons considered a knowledge of that language to be the crown of scholarship. We can see how this élitist programme of education became the basis of the English university and grammar school system which lasted for the next thousand years. 'The youngest of the king's sons,' Asser tells us,

> were to be educated with almost all the children of noble birth throughout the country, and even many of humbler birth. In the schools, books in both languages, that is, Latin and Saxon, were to be studied and time was set aside for writing. Accordingly the students were to become skilled in the liberal arts.[11]

Having by his own example and precept made learning the first priority, Alfred turned his attention to the law. But when about 893 he set about the enormous task of revising and supplementing the ancient codes of the Saxons, he found that the task of reconciling the heathen practices of his German ancestors and the teachings of Jesus Christ was beyond him, so it is no wonder that his attempts at codifying the law-book get bogged down in the *minutiae* of what should be the fine for cutting off a man's nose, ear, finger, or thumb; and what should be the financial penalty for knocking out a front and/or back tooth. He admits himself that he retained only those existing laws which pleased him personally, rejecting those which did not. And 'I did not dare to set down in writing many of my own suggestions, not knowing how they would be liked by those who should come after.'[12] What he means is that his concept of the law was basically that of his Saxon ancestors, despite his unquestioning devotion to the Christian faith. Yet it must have

[11] *The Chronicle*, p. 75.

[12] *The Laws of the Kings of England from Edmund to Henry I*. Edited by F. E. Harmer. Cambridge: University Press, 1914. p. 52.

seemed obvious to him that while turning the other cheek might be ideal in an ideal society, in the real world of Anglo-Saxon England, retribution was bound to be the basis of private justice. Hence Alfred's laws allowed a man the right to wage 'lawful war' against the seducer of his wife, sister, or mother. A complainant could also lay siege to an enemy's house for seven days and even slay him without guilt, provided he had first demanded justice of him. Forward-looking though he was and desiring greatly to civilize his people, Alfred could still see no way of overturning what his fellow aristocrats had for generations regarded as 'natural law'; and in the end he changed very little, apart from lowering the fines which were beginning to be substituted for blood-feuds. He did what he could to elevate the old conventions by insisting that all oaths and pledges must be kept; that men must be loyal to their lords and masters in order to achieve some kind of stability after centuries of wars; and that the poor and weak should be protected from abuse by the rich and strong. The laws framed to check violence to women were precise and enforceable. Provision was made for working men's holidays, their legal entitlement being thirty-six days in the year. It was the law-giving of a king who still regarded himself not as a symbolic head of state, but as the active head of a family, personally responsible for the well-being of all his subject-children. This was no posturing, for we have his views clearly stated in his will:

> I pray in the name of God and of His saints that none of my kinsmen or legatees oppress any of my dependants after my death. . . . And I desire for the love of God and for the good of my soul that they may be entitled to their freedom and to their choice. And I enjoin that no man put pressure upon them.[13]

[13] *Select English Historical Documents of the Ninth and Tenth Centuries*. Edited by F. E. Harmer. Cambridge: University Press, 1914. p. 52.

And like a tribal chieftain, Alfred expected complete loyalty from all his subjects, as well as loyalty from the lower to the higher orders – peasants to landowners, landowners to their lords, lords to their kings. The king and his thegns had taken the foremost part in fighting and eventually defeating the Danes and hence were entitled to special respect, like the head of a family. For the English people of this period were in a very material sense a large family whose welfare depended upon the experience, wisdom, and courage of their leaders. They were fortunate indeed in having a *paterfamilias* of Alfred's character, a king of such ability that he was statesman, soldier, legislator, scholar, architect, master-craftsman, and Defender of the Faith. It is fitting, too, that such a king should write his own epitaph: 'I may say that it has ever been my desire to live worthily and after my death to leave to them who will come after me my memorial in good works.'[14]

King Alfred died on October 29, 899, in the fifty-third year of his age and was buried in St Swithun's monastery at Winchester. In the reign of Henry I (1068–1135), his body was transported to a new tomb in Hyde Abbey, which, together with the other great monasteries of the land, was suppressed by Henry VIII. At the end of the eighteenth century, the authorities demolished the ruins of Hyde Abbey and erected a jail on the site. At that time the tombs were thrown down, the stone coffins turned into horse troughs, and the bones of kings and abbots scattered to the winds. As a result, nothing very tangible survives of our only monarch to be called *Great*; and for that matter very few secular monuments at all have come down to us from Anglo-Saxon times. The German tribes who invaded and colonized England from AD 450 to 600 were not builders, and when they did become to some extent urbanized, they had to call in continental architects and masons to erect the occasional stone building they required for public assemblies, notably

[14] W. J. Sedgefield, *King Alfred's Version of the Consolation of Boethius Done into Modern English*. London: Frowde, 1900. p. 212.

their churches. Such works as they did build have, with a few exceptions, disappeared, replaced in the case of their little churches, for instance, by splendid Norman cathedrals. Where, then, does the student go to see something tangible of those Saxons who laid the foundation of our nation, especially places personally associated with the more memorable kings?

Wantage is the birthplace of Alfred the Great. But this town in the Vale of the White Horse at the foot of the Berkshire Downs is so characterless in the fashion of contemporary commercial architecture that it takes a great effort of the imagination to visualize its royal origins. A vast car park where there was once a market place and village green going back to Saxon times does not encourage the amateur historian to linger in Wantage. Similarly, Winchester in Hampshire is not readily recognizable as the great king's legislative capital; and since the Church of St Swithun where both he and King Canute were entombed was demolished to make a site for the Norman cathedral, Winchester belongs more to the mediaeval than to the Saxon period.

The most famous, as well as the most neglected of the places associated with Alfred – the Isle of Athelney – is well worth a visit, even though the visitor will not find a stone left of the great king's bridge, fort, and monastery. Yet no place in England can evoke the sense of his presence so effectively as the Somerset marshes. In Saxon times, Athelney was an actual island which could only be reached by boat, though there is mention in contemporary reports of a bridge connecting the surrounding country with a fort built by Alfred as his headquarters during the campaigns of AD 878 against the Danes. Here it was that he planned the liberation of his kingdom; and here, in thanks for his success, he founded a monastery dedicated to Our Blessed Saviour. If only we could see as much of Alfred's monastery as was visible in the seventeenth century! For though Henry VIII dissolved Athelney, drove out the monks, and sold all the lands to speculators, some buildings did survive until 1674 when they were systematically knocked down by a certain Captain

Hacker, with no attempt to record the site and the artefacts found thereon. Twenty years later the discovery nearby of 'King Alfred's Jewel', one of the most sensational events in British archaeology, alerted antiquarians to the importance of the region, for this unique artefact, now in the Ashmolean Museum, Oxford, is the only surviving relic of Alfred's sojourn in the Somerset wilderness. The jewel is inscribed AELFRED MEC HEHT GEWYRCAN ('Alfred ordered me to be made') and consists of a miniature of a seated figure enamelled on a gold plate protected by a surround of rock crystal, the whole contained within a gold frame of delicately executed filigree work.

The Isle of Athelney, which is now identified with the twin hillocks about four miles south-west of Bridgewater, is in the centre of the fenland formed by Salt Moor, Stan Moor, Allen Moor, Lying Moor, and so on – to-day rich dairy land, in Alfred's time a wilderness of marsh and forest abounding in game, especially the red deer which survived in the wild until the beginning of this century. The fact of its lying off the main transportation routes gives it a special character, so that it is not difficult for the explorer to see Athelney as William of Malmesbury described it in 1125:

> The monastery of Athelney with the cells of the monks is situated on two small hillocks in the marsh. It was built by King Alfred in thanksgiving for his having driven the Danes from his kingdom. He rebuilt the existing hermitage [of St Ethelwin, the seventh-century hermit who dwelt here] in the new style. The new structure was supported on four pillars and had four round enclosures for use as cloisters. To-day Athelney has a few impoverished monks, but their needs are few and they are quite content to live in solitude.[15]

[15] Willelmi Malmesbiriensis Monachi, *De Gestis Pontificum Anglorum*. Translated by James Wellard. London: Longman & Co., 1870. p. 199.

OFFA'S DYKE: from the Irish Sea to the Bristol Channel

Guidebook: *Offa's Dyke.* A Walker's Guide. London: Ministry of Works, 1979.

An agreeable headquarters for the exploration of this famous earthworks is Montgomery in Montgomeryshire. Situated about halfway along Offa's Dyke, this Welsh town is itself a microcosm of early British history, epitomized in the now ruined castle built by the Norman knight Baldwin in 1070. From Montgomery there is a short walk to a well-preserved section of the Dyke at Rownal Covert from whence one can look westwards, as Offa's sentries must have done 1200 years ago to the ancient British (i.e. Welsh) kingdoms of Gwent, Powys, Dyfed, and Gwynedd.

The Dyke was built during the reign of Offa, king of Mercia (752–96). It is approximately 149 miles long and roughly follows the present Welsh-English border. Its northern terminal is on the Irish Sea, its southern on the Bristol Channel. Originally it had an average height of about six feet and a width of fifty feet. It was not a continuous barrier like Hadrian's Wall and did not have to be, since the builders were able to take advantage of every river, ravine, and forest along the north-south line so that in theory there was no stretch of undefended frontier between the kingdom of Mercia to the east and the Welsh kingdoms to the west.

Who was the king who had the resources to build such a monument? Why and how was this immense barrier erected?

The king was Offa, an East Saxon chieftain who, like many of his counterparts, created a kingdom by first killing his domestic rivals and then invading the neighbouring states. Though claiming direct descent from Woden and steeped in the old pagan culture, he adopted the outward mode of the Christian kings, even to his formal submission to the Church. By 788, he had made himself overlord of all England south of the Humber and so became the first of the Saxon chiefs to proclaim himself,

26 Offa's Dyke, named after the eighth-century king of Mercia who built it, runs some 149 miles in a north-south direction from the Irish Sea to the Bristol Channel. It was intended to form a frontier between Anglo-Saxon England and British Wales. What remains of part of this earth-wall can be seen in this aerial photograph as a white line.

with some justification, *rex anglorum* and *rex anglorum patriae.* Offa can be compared with Alfred the Great in that his prestige extended well beyond his own dominion to the kingdoms of Europe. But in all other respects he was the antithesis of Alfred, for he had little of the goodness, intelligence, and nobility of the West Saxon king, and his continuous wars were wars of conquests, not of liberation. It was his unsuccessful attempts to subdue the old British-Romano principalities of Wales which led to the erection of his Dyke, a great earth barrier in imitation of Hadrian's stone wall and, like that monument, meant to mark the limits of his conquests.

The military engineers who supervised the project had problems which would tax the skills of technical experts to-day. While the Dyke builders could and did make use of natural defensive features, like the river Severn in the centre and a dense forest protecting forty-seven miles at the southern end of the line, they were unable to build a bank higher than six feet anywhere along the rampart on account of the wet, alluvial soil of the Welsh marshes. They compensated for the lack of height by broadening the bank and deepening the ditches, the work being carried out over many years by gangs of prisoners and slaves, though it is still incredible where Offa found sufficient manpower to shift hundreds of thousands of tons of earth.

The enthusiast with plenty of time and a stout pair of boots can, with the aid of a large-scale Survey map, still follow the Dyke along much of its length, although only a few sections remain relatively intact.

YORK: the Danish Kingdom, AD 866–1066

Guidebook: Shannon, John, *Historic York*. Norwich: Jarrold, 1978.

Perhaps no other city illustrates the *diversity* of English history so vividly as this ancient capital of Northumbria. As *Eboracum*, it was one of the most important centres of Roman Britain, serving as GHQ for the 9th and 6th Legions and even becoming for three years during the reign of the emperor Severus a sort of provincial capital of the Empire.

A 'ghost town' after the departure of the Roman administra-

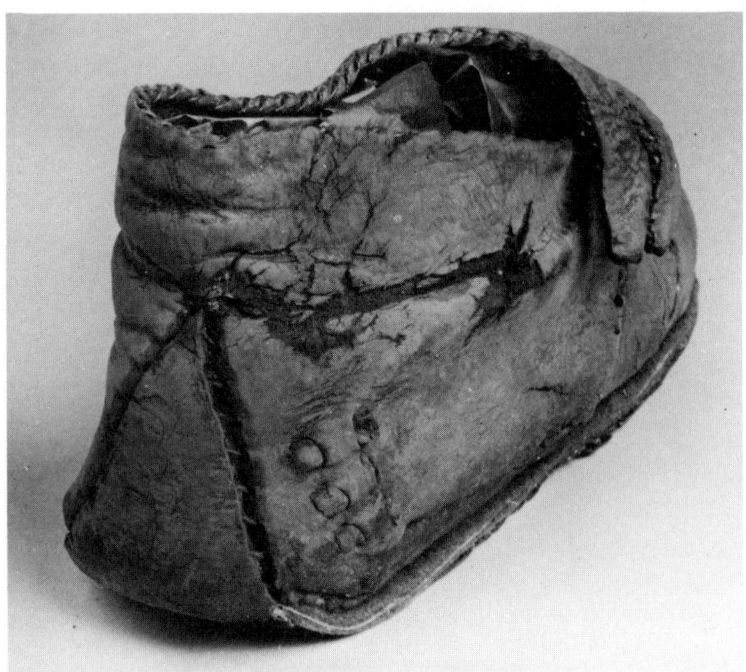

27 A leather shoe, a sock, and a storage jar (*right*) were a few of the finds of recent excavations of Viking York. Such humble articles of everyday life tell historians a great deal about the Danish colony of Jervik, founded in 866 and lasting about 200 years.

tors, though with its walls, fortress, temples, and public buildings still intact, York disappears from the written records until it becomes the capital of the Anglian Kingdom of Northumbria about AD 550.

The known history of *Eoforvic*, as it was now called, begins with King Aethelfrith who reigned 24 years (593–617). This man with his two wives and numerous concubines was one of the last of the pagan kings of England; and though he slaughtered 1,200 monks at the Battle of Chester ('If they are calling on their God against us, they are fighting against us, if not with arms, then with curses'), the Venerable Bede calls him 'a most valiant king'.

Aethelfrith's successors were converted to Christianity, and by the eighth century York was enjoying a Golden Age as the centre of learning, literature, and the arts. Here Archbishop Egbert, brother of King Aedberht, founded the famous school and assembled one of the greatest libraries of the West. Here, too, was born the brilliant scholar Ealhwine who was to become internationally famous as Alcuin, the friend and counsellor of Charlemagne.

The reign of York as the cultural capital of England was abruptly ended by a Danish warlord called Hafdan. Hafdan was a leader of the Great Army which landed in East Anglia in 865, captured York a year later, and founded the kingdom of Jervik with its own kings, laws, and language. York and the surrounding countryside was now a Danish colony which lasted for nearly 200 years under fifteen successive kings, and is still remembered in many Yorkshire place names and a whole vocabulary of borrowed words. *Window*, *husband*, and *bread* are verbal relics of the Kingdom of Jervik, whose last ruler was Eric Bloodaxe, son of Harold Fairhair, king of Norway.

The wealth of this Danish state was derived from international trade. Excavations of the last five years have uncovered a commercial centre inhabited by merchants who, judging from the variety and provenance of the artefacts found on the site, had dealings with their Scandinavian confrères all over Europe and the East. Coins from Tashkent and Samarkand indicate what an important emporium Jervik had become by the tenth century, for the Viking world to which the city now belonged was international.

The site of the Danish merchant community in York was for a long time open to the public, but has now been closed. But the rich haul of finds – notably of domestic articles – has been handsomely housed in the Museum, providing a vivid picture of the life and times of this unique outpost of Anglo-Saxon England.

York's last link with the period is King Harold who fought long and hard to defend his kingdom against invaders. Early in

1066 he defeated the army of King Hardrada of Norway just outside York at Stamford Bridge. It was while he was celebrating his victory in one of the great halls of the city that a messenger brought the news of the Norman invasion on the Sussex coast, 300 miles away. The date was October 1st, 1066. Three weeks later Harold was dead. He was the last of the Saxon kings, and with his death the Anglo-Saxon period was ended. The new era can be seen in the Norman architecture which dominates York to-day – William the Conqueror's two massive castles; the great Minster begun in 1079; and the King's Manor, formerly St Mary's Abbey, founded in 1089.

BOSHAM (Sussex): Remembrances of Saxon England

Guidebook: *Historic Bosham*, Festival Guide. Croydon: Home Publishing Co. [1951].

The small creek village of Bosham (pronounced Bozzum) three miles west of Chichester is an example of an English community continuously inhabited since Roman times which has managed to retain its identity. Tourism has not yet affected Bosham, the historic buildings have not been demolished to make way for car parks, and one age is allowed to merge imperceptibly into the next – Roman into Saxon, Saxon into Norman, Norman into mediaeval, and so up to the age of the weekend yachtsman. Bosham is as English to-day as it was when King Harold worshipped in the church portrayed on the Bayeux Tapestry – the same church from whose Saxon tower the bells still ring out across the Sussex landscape of creeks and water-meadows.

In Roman days (and until quite recently), Bosham was a settlement of fishermen and oystermen who supplied the market of the nearby town of *Noviomagus* (Chichester). It was also, as it still is, a summer resort, and some credence can be given to the tradition that the Emperor Vespasian had a villa here in

28 The Bayeux Tapestry's picture of Bosham Church as it looked in 1064. King Harold is shown entering the church before embarking for Normandy. The chancel arch survives in its original Saxon form. (*Below*) Harold feasts in a mansion which probably belonged to King Canute whose little daughter, drowned in the nearby creek, is said to be buried in Bosham Church.

view of the considerable Roman remains found within the village precincts, notably a life-sized marble head of the first century AD.

But it is as an Old English settlement that Bosham is especially important, since the last monument of the South Saxon Kingdom is found here. This kingdom, which was pagan until the conversion of an obscure king named Aelhelwalh, was once dotted with abbeys, churches (adjacent Selsey had its own cathedral, now said to be under the sea), and royal residences. The one surviving building from this South Saxon world is the Holy Trinity Church at Bosham.

The church, which has been renovated through the years, may have been built on the site of a Roman basilica of the fourth century. The unusual heavy masonry, together with the characteristic bricks and tiles bonded into the walls, are undoubtedly Roman. Alternatively, the foundations are on or near the site of a hermitage established in Bosham by an Irish monk named Dicul. This Dicul had come to Sussex in the seventh century with the mission of converting the pagan South Saxons who had spread all along the coast and into the Isle of Wight. He chose Bosham for his headquarters – an indication of its importance; and here he founded a monastery served by six brothers. But he appears to have had little success in converting the heathen, for according to Bede 'none of the natives cared for his preaching'. Some traces of Dicul's cell were said to be visible in 1635 when the antiquary John Smythe visited Bosham and was shown ruins by 'the inhabitants who derive their knowledge of tradition from their forefathers'.

The church was built for a secular as well as a religious purpose. The massive tower with its original small Saxon windows was designed as a 'look-out' and refuge, for Bosham was frequently attacked by Viking pirates throughout the Anglo-Saxon period and was pillaged even during the reign of King Canute (1016–35).

The village is especially associated with this Danish King who was supposed to have had a *vill*, or royal residence, where now stands the Manor House on the banks of the mill stream. Canute, says the legend, sat himself on a chair and commanded the waves to recede. Anyone who has seen what the sea is like along this stretch of coast when a south-west gale meets the ebb tide will either question the king's sanity or accept the ingenious explanation of local antiquarians that Canute built earthworks (still called 'chairs') along Bosham Creek to protect the fields, and when the tide was contained within the banks, he was fulsomely congratulated by his courtiers for commanding the sea itself.

The discovery in 1865 of a stone coffin containing the bones of a five-year-old girl under a slab by the chancel seemed to confirm the tradition that King Canute's little daughter had been drowned in Bosham Creek and buried in the church. A sepulchre in the north wall of the chancel containing the recumbent effigy of a child with feet resting upon the body of a lion is now thought to be part of the Canute Memorial. The chancel arch itself, one of the finest examples of Saxon architecture, is well depicted in the Bayeux Tapestry which shows Harold and his companions riding to Bosham, the king with a hawk on his wrist. The king worshipped in the church (presumably leaving his hawk outside) before sailing across the Channel to Normandy from Bosham Quay. The village with its church, manor house, fishermen's cottages, and souvenirs of saints and kings is a direct link, one of very few, with Anglo-Saxon England.

EPILOGUE

This book is called by the natives Domesday – that is, metaphorically, the Day of Judgment. For as the sentence of that strict and terrible account cannot be evaded by any skilful subterfuge, so when this book is appealed to on those matters which it contains its sentence cannot be quashed or set aside with impunity.

Richard fitz Nigel,
the Treasurer of England, writing in
the year 1179

In the year 1085, says *The Anglo-Saxon Chronicle*, 'at Gloucester at midwinter, King William held his court five days. And after this he had a great council and very deep speech with his councillors about this land, how it was peopled and by what sort of persons. He then sent his men all over England into every shire to find out what or how much each landowner held in land and livestock, and what it was worth. So very narrowly he caused it to be traced out that there was not one yard of land nor even – it is a shame to tell, though it seemed to him no shame to do it – an ox, or cow, or pig was omitted from his survey.'[1]

The Norman was thorough. One of his councillors at this conference in Gloucester, Robert Losinga, Bishop of Hereford, records that a second team of investigators followed the first, and secret agents were sent into the provinces to check up on the reports of their predecessors.

Historians have called the Domesday Book the most remark-

[1] *The Anglo-Saxon Chronicle*. Translated by Benjamin Thorpe. London: Longmans, Green, 1861. Vol. ii, p. 186.

able statistical document in European history. It is more than statistical. It is the document that symbolized the end of an era which began with the discovery of these islands by Pytheas in the fifth century BC and ended 1500 years later with the emergence of the England we know to-day. Any entry in the Domesday Book, even one chosen at random, illustrates this thesis. The underlying concept of the survey is *modern* in the sense that from the moment this national census was undertaken, central government began monitoring practically every aspect of a citizen's life. For as the scribe of *The Anglo-Saxon Chronicle* tells us, the king now knew not only who was who, who lived where, how much he owned, and what he did, but what was his social status and hence his rights or obligations. An examination of the data given in the Commissioners Report for the London borough of Chelsea as it was in 1086 will confirm this:

> Edward of Salisbury owns 240 acres in the Manor of Chelsea.
> There is land available for cultivation by five ploughteams.*
> The Lord of the Manor owns 120 acres. Two teams are now working there.
> The villagers are cultivating as much land as one team can work, but two more teams could be employed.
> Two of the villagers own thirty acres apiece.
> Four own 7½ acres.
> Three smallholders own 5 acres.
> Three slaves [live in the village].
> There are 200 acres of meadow, pasture for village livestock, woods, and 60 pigs.
> Total value of the Manor of Chelsea, £9 when bought and no change since.
> Wulfwen was the freeholder of this manor. She could sell to whom she pleased.[2]

* A *ploughteam* (caruca) consisted of a plough drawn by eight oxen.

[2] Adapted from *Domesday Book* 11. Middlesex: p. 20 *Ossulstone Hundred*. Chichester: Phillimore, 1975. p. 130c,d.

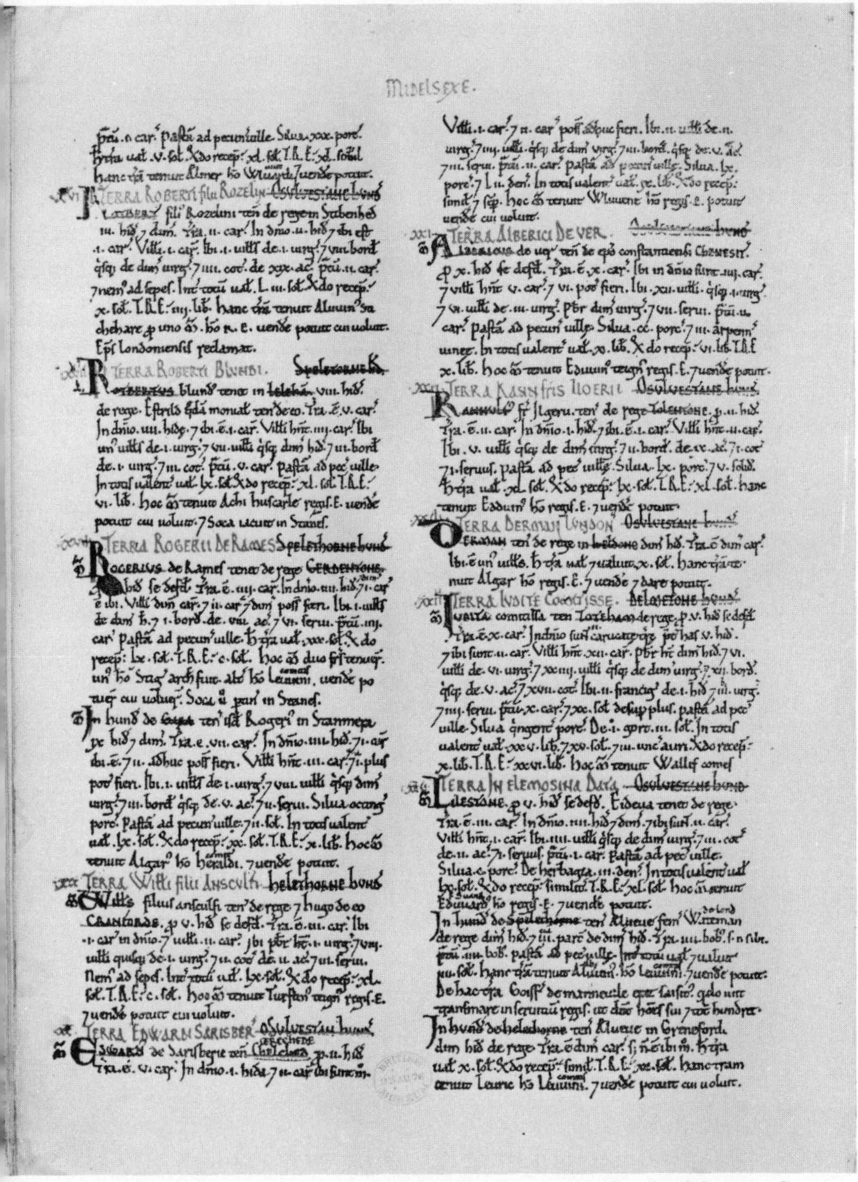

29 A page from the Domesday Book with the entry for the Manor of Chelsea, whose total value is assessed at £9. The entry begins at the bottom of the left-hand column with the words TERRA EDWARDI.

When all the thousands of facts about the social and economic condition of England are collated, it becomes obvious that the disorganized and fragmented England of Offa and Alfred, of Canute and Harold, belongs almost to the nation's prehistory. Thegns and ceorls are suddenly as foreign sounding as the consuls and legates of Roman Britannia. Clearly England was now to be under entirely new management. Norman lords, not Saxon earls, made the rules, both political and social. Ended were the perpetual feuds between petty chieftains and the major wars which had gone on for hundreds of years between kings. Ended, too, was the greatest threat of all to the national security, the invasion of the heathen Norsemen, nowadays idealized under the title of Vikings, but regarded by their contemporaries as barbarians who lived by murder and looting. The Anglo-Saxons were soon to become Anglo-Normans, speaking a new language and adopting a new culture. The age of the house-carl who fought at Hastings with a sling was over; that of the knight on horseback had begun.

But the fundamental change in the life of the nation was manifested in literature, art, architecture, music, and manners. One has only to compare the sound and content of an Anglo-Saxon epic like *Beowulf* with an Anglo-Norman romance like *Sir Gawain and the Green Knight* to sense that change. The mead-hall, where drinking thegns had roared their approval of Beowulf's slaughter of Grendel in hand-to-hand combat, was soon to be replaced by the castle where knights and ladies listened to the story of the attempted seduction of Gawain by his hostess and his acceptance of her kisses and her girdle.

The revolution had been brought about by a Norman baron originally known as William the Bastard but now remembered as William the Conqueror, a freebooter who seized the throne of England by force and retained it by terror, a man whose lust for power made him impervious to human suffering. It was this illegitimate son of a tanner who united the tribes of Britons, Celts, Angles, Saxons, Jutes, and Scandinavians and laid the foundations of a nation which was to conquer and rule one-third of the globe. So in the eleventh century was born the Britain we first hear of as 'The Pretanic Isles', an archipelago on the edge of the Ocean, a mythical land, and one that is becoming more difficult every year to believe ever existed at all, let alone to discover. In attempting to do so, I have tried to remember the *apologia* of one of our first historians, the Welsh monk Nennius:

> I have got together all that I could from the annals and from our own ancient traditions. Many teachers and scribes have attempted to do this, but somehow or other have abandoned the task on account of its difficulty. I pray that every reader who shall read this book may pardon me for having attempted to write these things. But I was uneasy lest the name of my people, formerly famous and distinguished, should sink into oblivion and, like smoke, pass away and vanish.[3]

[3] Nennius. *The History of the Britons.* From *Old English Chronicles.* Bohn's Antiquarian Library. London: George Bell, 1908. p. 383.

30 William Camden (1551–1623), the English antiquary and author of *Britannia*, who set out in 1580 'to acquaint the world with the ancient state of Britain'.

BIBLIOGRAPHY

Those readers who have become interested in some special aspect of the Unknown Britain described in this book will find the following bibliography helpful, provided they have access to a large library. Unfortunately most of the older histories are out of print and the monographs describing particular sites are buried away in the journals of regional archaeological societies; but the Department of the Environment, H. M. Stationery Office, publishes guide-books to all the major historic sites in the British Isles, and these guides together with the Ordnance Survey maps will be invaluable aids to the enthusiast. One can start with *Historic Monuments in the care of the State and open to the Public* (H. M. Stationery Office) in which the reader will find archaeological sites listed by counties, with information regarding their locations, hours of admission, and so on.

In addition to the Department of the Environment's large and easily available stock of books, the county and town museums invariably have an excellent selection of specialized guides usually written by a local historian. Armed with these books, the traveller is ready to explore a Britain which still keeps traces of our history going back at least four thousand years.

Chapter 1. THE DISCOVERY OF THE PRETANIC ISLES

Aoust, L. X. B., *Études sur Pytheas*. Paris: Gauthier-Villars, 1866

Barry, George, *History of the Orkneys*. London: Longman, Hurst, Rees & Orme, 1808

Bowley, Ernest Lyon, *The Fortunate Islands*. St Mary's, Scilly: the Author, 1954

Bulleid, Arthur, *The Lake Villages*. London: The Folk Press, 1924

Cary, M. and Warmington, E. H., *The Ancient Explorers*. London: Methuen, 1929

Charton, Édouard, *Pytheas: Navigation depuis Marseilles jusqu'à Thule*. Paris: Bureau du Magasin Pittoresque, 1854.

Childe, V. G., *Prehistoric Communities of the British Isles*. London and Edinburgh: Chambers, 1949

———, *Prehistory of Scotland*. London: Bell, 1935

Christison, David, *Early Fortifications in Scotland*. Edinburgh & London: Blackwood, 1898.

Clark, E. V., *Cornish Fogous*. London: Methuen, 1961

Crawford, O. G. S., 'Lyonesse'. *Antiquity*, I (1927)

Cunliffe, B. W., *Iron Age Communities in Britain*. London: Routledge, 1974

Davies, Edward, *Celtic Researches*. London: printed by the Author, 1804

Dudley, David, 'Bodrifty'. *Archaeological Journal*, cxiii (1956)

Edmonds, Richard, *The Land's End District*. Penzance: printed by the Author, 1862

Elton, Charles Isaac, *Origins of English History*. London: Quaritch, 1890

Excavations at Maen Castle. Proceedings of the West Cornish Field Club, I, 3 (1953–55); II, 3 (1959)

Fox, Sir Cyril F., *A Find of the Early Iron Age from Llyn Cerrig Bach*. Cardiff: National Museum of Wales, 1946

———, *The Personality of Britain*. Cardiff: National Museum of Wales, 1952

Fox, J. P. Bushe-, *Excavations at Hengistbury Head, Hampshire*. London: O.U.P., 1915

Fulton, Thomas, 'Grimes Graves'. *Journal of the Ethnological Society*, New Series ii (1870)

Hamilton, J. R. C., *Excavations at Jarlshof, Shetland*. Ministry of Works, Archaeological Reports, No. 1

Handbook of West Cornwall. London: Nattali, 1872

Harden, Donald B., *Dark Age Britain*. London: Methuen, 1956

Hawkes, C. F. C., 'Hill Forts'. *Antiquity*, V (1931)

Hencken, Hugh O'Neill, *The Archaeology of Cornwall*. London: Methuen, 1932

———, 'Chysauster'. *Archaeologia*, lxxxiii (1933)

Holmes, T. R. E., *Ancient Britain and the Invasion of Julius Caesar*. London: O.U.P., 1936

Jesson, M. and Hill, D., *The Iron Age and its Hill Forts*. Southampton: University Press, 1971

Kendrick, T. D., *The Druids*. London: Methuen, 1921

Kershaw, Nora (ed.), *Studies in Early British History*. Cambridge: U.P., 1954

Laing, L. R., *Orkney and Shetland: an Archaeological Guide*. Newton Abbot: David and Charles, 1974

Lelewel, Joachim, *Pytheas de Marseille*. Paris: Straszewicz, 1836

Mackie, Euan W., 'The Origin and Development of the Broch . . . of the Scottish Iron Age'. *Proceedings*, Prehistoric Society, xxxi (1965)

Markham, Sir John, 'Pytheas, Discoverer of Britain'. *Geographical Journal*, June, 1893

Mercer, R., 'Carn Brea'. *Cornish Archaeology*, ix, x, xi (1970–2)

Murray, John, *Handbook for Travellers in Cornwall*. London: Murray, 1893

Posidonius, *The Histories*. Edited by L. Edelstein and I. G. Kidd. Cambridge: U.P., 1972

Tierney, J. T., 'The Celtic Ethnography of Posidonius'. *Proceedings*, Royal Irish Academy, Vol. 60, Section C, No. 5 (1962)

Turnbull, C. M., *The Forest People*. London: Chatto and Windus, 1961

Vale, H. E. T., *Ancient England*. London: Batsford, 1941

Wheeler, R. E. M., 'Maiden Castle, Dorset'. Society of Antiquaries, *Report No. 12* (1937)

Chapter 2. THE PHOENICIANS IN BRITAIN

Barnett, R. D., 'Early Shipping in the Near East'. *Antiquity*, xxxii (1958)

Basch, L., 'Phoenician Oared Ships'. *Mariners' Mirror*, LV, 2 and 3 (1951)

Bérard, Victor, *Les Phéniciens et l'Odysée*. Paris: A. Colin, 1927

Bonsor, George, *Tartesse*. New York: The Hispanic Society, 1922

Charles-Picard, Gilbert, *Daily Life in Carthage at the Time of Hannibal*. London: Allen and Unwin, 1961

Contenau, George, *La Civilization phénicienne*. Paris: Payot, 1926

Culican, William, *The First Merchant Venturers*. London: Thames & Hudson, 1966

Edmonds, Richard, *The Phoenician Tin Trade*. Plymouth: The Institution, 1866

Février, J. G., 'L'Ancienne Marine phénicienne'. *La Nouvelle Clio*, III (1950)

Harden, Donald, *The Phoenicians*. London: Thames & Hudson, 1971

Hawkins, Christopher, *The Tin Trade of the Ancients*. Truro: the Author, 1821

Holmes, T. R. E., *Ancient Britain*. London: O.U.P., 1936

Laing, L. R., 'A Greek Tin Trade with Cornwall'. *Cornish Archaeology*, 7 (1968)
Matthews, G. F., *The Isles of Scilly*. London: Ronald, 1960
Rogers, Clara C., *The Scilly Isles*. London: Hale, 1953
Smith, George L., *The Cassiterides*. London: Murray, 1863
Taylor, E. G. R., *The Haven-finding Art*. London: Hollis & Carter, 1971
Taylor, Thomas, *St Michael's Mount*. Cambridge: U.P., 1932
Truro, Royal Institution. *Guide to the County Museum*. Truro, 1966
Weill, Raymond, *Phoenicia*. London: Harrap, 1940

Chapter 3. BRITANNIA FELIX

Atkinson, Donald, 'The Classis Britannica'. *Historical Essays in Honour of James Tait*. Manchester: U.P., 1933
Ausonius, Decimus Magnus, *Works*. Translated by H. G. E. White. London: Heinemann, 1919
Avienus, Rufus Festus, *Description de la Terre*. Tr. by MM Despois et Saviot. Paris: Panckouke, 1843
Bick, David E., *The Old Metal Mines of Mid-Wales*. Newent: Pound House, 1974
Birley, Anthony, *Life in Roman Britain*. London: Batsford, 1964
Boon, George C., *Isca: a Guide*. Cardiff: Nat. Mus. of Wales, 1960
———, *Roman Silchester*. London: Max Parrish, 1957
Bromehead, C. E. C., 'Roman Mines'. *Antiquity*, xvi (1942)
Bruce, John Collingwood, *Handbook to the Roman Wall*. Newcastle: Hindson & Andrew Reid, 1966
Burn, A. R., *The Romans in Britain: an Anthology of Inscriptions*. London: Blackwell, 1969
Bury, J. B., 'Notitia Dignitatum'. *Journal of Roman Studies*, x (1920)
Caesar, Julius, *The Gallic Wars*. Penguin Classics, no. L 21
Celsus, Aulus Cornelius, *Of Medicine*. Tr. by J. Gregory. London: Chidley, 1837
Chadwick, N. K., *Poetry and Letters in Early Christian Gaul*. London: Bowes & Bowes, 1955
Codrington, Thomas, *Roman Roads in Britain*. London: S.P.C.K., 1918
Cunliffe, Barry, 'Portchester Castle'. Portsmouth: *The Portsmouth Papers*, No. 1 (1967)
Davies, O., *Roman Mines in Europe*. Oxford: Clarendon Press, 1935
Diodorus Siculus, *The Historical Library*. Tr. by Henry Parks. London: J. Davis, 1814

Fastidius, *Works*. Tr. by R. S. T. Hazelhurst. London: Society of SS Peter and Paul, 1927

Glover, T. R., *Life and Letters in the Fourth Century*. Cambridge: U.P., 1901

Gough, J. W., *The Mines of Mendip*. Newton Abbot: David & Charles, 1967

Hull, M. R., *Roman Colchester*, Oxford: U.P., 1958

Jackson, Kenneth, *Language in Early Britain*. Edinburgh: U.P., 1953

———, 'On the Vulgar Latin of Roman Britain'. *Mediaeval Studies in Honor of J. D. M. Ford*. Cambridge, Mass: U.P., 1948

Lindsay, Jack, *The Romans Were Here*. London: Muller, 1956

Margary, Ivan D., *Roman Roads in Britain*. London: Baker, 1973

Parker, H. M. *The Roman Legions*. Oxford: Clarendon Press, 1958

Phillips, C. W., *The Fenland in Roman Times*. London: Royal Geographical Research Series, No. 5 (1970)

Pratt, J. H., 'Portchester'. *Antiquaries' Journal*, xlix (1969)

Querolus; or Aulularia. A Late Drama in Latin by a Gaul. Tr. by Léon Herrman. Bruxelles: B. Demarez, 1937

Richmond, I. A., *Roman Britain*. London: Cape, 1963

Rivet, A. F. L., *Town and Country in Roman Britain*. London: Hutchinson, 1966

Rodwell, W., and Rowley, T. (eds.) *Small Towns of Roman Britain*. Oxford: U.P., 1975

Scarborough, John, *Roman Medicine*. London: Thames & Hudson, 1969

Solinus, Caius Julius, *The Excellent & Pleasant Worke*. Gainesville, Fla.: Scholars' Reprints, 1955

Starr, Chester G., *The Roman Imperial Navy*. Ithaca, N.Y.: Cornell U.P., 1941

Tacitus, Cornelius, *Annals*. Tr. by Henry Furneaux. London: Murray, 1959

———, *Life of Agricola*. Tr. by J. Aikin. London: Taylor, 1904

Wacher, J. S., *The Towns of Roman Britain*. London: Batsford, 1974

Webster, Graham, *The Roman Army*. London: Black, 1969

Williams, Hugh, *Christianity in Early Britain*. Oxford: Clarendon Press, 1912

Wilson, R. J. A., *A Guide to Roman Remains in Britain*. London: Constable, 1980

Chapter 4. GODS AND GHOSTS: THE RELIGIONS OF ROMAN BRITAIN

Allen, J. R. and Anderson, J., *The Early Christian Monuments of Scotland*. Edinburgh: Neill & Co., 1903

Barley, M. W. and Hanson, R. P. C. (eds), *Christianity in Britain*. Leicester: U.P., 1968

Book of Lismore. Edited by Whitley Stokes. Oxford: U.P., 1890

Collingwood, R. G., 'The Roman Evacuation of Britain'. *Journal of Roman Studies*, xii (1922)

Cunliffe, Barry, *Roman Bath*. London: Society of Antiquaries, 1969

Doble, G. H., *St Illtut*. Cardiff: U. of Wales Press, 1944

Gildas, *Works*. Tr. by J. A. Giles. London: J. Bohn, 1841

Gillam, J. P., 'The London Mithraeum'. *Journal of Roman Studies*, xlv (1955) and xivi (1956).

Gould, Sabine and John Baring, *The Lives of the British Saints*. London: Cymmrodonon Society, 1907–13

Lewis, M. J. T., *Temples in Roman Britain*. Cambridge: U.P., 1966

Little, B. D. G., *Bath Portrait*. London: Collins, 1961

Meates, G. W., *Lullingstone Roman Villa*. London: Heinemann, 1955

Nennius, *History of the Britons*. Tr. by A. W. Wade-Evans. London: Church Historical Society, 1938

Radford, C. A. R., *Tintagel Castle*. H. M. Office of Works Official Guides, 1939

Reed, T. D., *Battle for Britain in the Fifth Century*. London: Methuen, 1944

Richmond, I. A. and Gillam, J. P., 'The Temple of Mithras at Carrawburgh'. *Archaeologia Aeliana*, ser. 4, vol. 31 (1951)

Ross, A., *Pagan Celtic Britain*. London: Routledge & Kegan Paul, 1967

Rutilius Namatianus Claudius, *De Reditu Suo*. Tr. by J. W. Duff. London: Heinemann, 1934

Thevenot, E., *Divinités et Sanctuaires de la Gaulle*. Paris: Panckouke, 1968

Toynbee, J. M. C., 'Christianity in Roman Britain'. *Journal of the British Archaeological Association*, 3rd ser., xvi (1953)

Trewin, J. C., *The Story of Bath*. London: Staples Press, 1951

Vermaseren, M. J., *The Excavations in the Mithraeum of the Church of Saint Prisca in Rome*. Leiden: E. J. Brill, 1965

Williams, V. E. N., *The Early Christian Monuments of Wales*. Cardiff: U. of Wales Press, 1950

Chapter 5. THE GROANS OF THE BRITONS

Asser, Joannes Menevensis, *Life of King Alfred.* Edited by W. H. Stevenson. Oxford: U.P., 1959

Barrow, G. W., *Feudal Britain.* London: Arnold, 1956

Benson, G., *York from its Origin to the Eleventh Century.* York: Cooper & Swann, 1911

Beowulf. Tr. by Thomas Arnold. London: Longmans, 1876

Bone, G., *Anglo-Saxon Poetry.* Oxford: Clarendon Press, 1943

Bosham, Historic. Croydon: Home Publishing Co., 1951

Bosham. *A Walk round a Saxon Church.* Bosham: privately printed, 1955

Bowen, E. G., *The Settlements of the Celtic Saints in Wales.* Cardiff: U. of Wales Press, 1954

Chambers, R., *England before the Norman Conquest.* London: Longmans, 1932

Chatfield, A. L., *A History of Bosham and its Church.* Chichester: Meere and Wingham, 1939

Clapham, A. W., *English Romanesque Architecture before the Conquest.* Oxford: Clarendon Press, 1930

Cook, A. S. and Tinker, C. B., *Select Translations of Old English Poetry.* Cambridge, Mass.: Harvard U.P., 1935

Cramp, R. J., *Anglian and Viking York.* York: St Antony's Press, 1967

Fox, Sir Cyril F., *Offa's Dyke.* London: O.U.P., 1955

Gildas, *Works.* Tr. by J. A. Giles. London: J. Bohm, 1841

Harden, D. B., (ed.), *Dark Age Britain.* London: Methuen, 1956

Hodgkin, R. H., *A History of the Anglo-Saxons.* London: O.U.P., 1953

Ker, W. M. P., *The Dark Ages.* London: Nelson, 1955

Lawlor, R. C., *The Monastery of St Mochasi.* Belfast: Belfast Natural History and Philosophical Society, 1925

Loewe, R., (ed.), 'The Commentary of Herbertus de Boseham'. *Biblica,* vol 34, fasc. 1 (1953)

Lot, Ferdinand, *The End of the Ancient World and the Beginnings of the Middle Ages.* London: Kegan Paul, 1951

Mahr, Adolf, *Christian Art in Ancient Ireland.* Dublin: Royal Irish Academy, 1932

Michel, F. X., *De Gestis Herewardi Saxonis.* Rouen: E. Frère, 1836

Radford, C. A. R., *Excavations at Whithorn: Final Report.* Transactions of the Dumfriesshire & Galloway Natural History Society, vol. 34 (1956)

Sidonius Apollinaris, *Poems and Letters*. Tr. by W. B. Anderson. London: Heinemann, 1936

Simpson, W. D., *St Ninian and the Origins of the Christian Church in Scotland*. Edinburgh: Oliver & Boyd, 1940

Stenton, D. M., *English Society in the Early Middle Ages*. Pelican Books, no. A 252 (1965)

Thomas, C., *Excavations at Whithorn*. Transactions of the Dumfries-shire & Galloway Natural History Society, vol. 38 (1960)

Chapter 6. HEATHEN KINGS AND CHRISTIAN SAINTS

Allen, J. R. and Anderson, J., *The Early Christian Monuments of Scotland*. Edinburgh: Society of Antiquities of Scotland, 1903

Boyle, John, *Portrait of Canterbury*. London: Hale, 1974

Caedmon, *Poems*. Tr. by C. W. Kennedy. London: Routledge, 1916

Chadwick, H. M., *The Origin of the English Nation*. Cambridge: U.P., 1907

Chadwick, N. K., *The Age of the Saints*. Oxford: U.P., 1961

———, *Celt and Saxon*. Cambridge: U.P., 1963

Felix, *Life of St. Guthlac*. Tr. by C. W. Goodwin. London: J. R. Smith, 1848

Finchale Priory: a Guide. Durham: G. M. Watt, 1887

Godric, Saint, *The Hymns*. Ed. by J. W. Rankin. Washington: Modern Language Association of America, 1923

Green, John R., *Conquest of England*. London: Macmillan, 1883

The Guthlac Roll. London: Roxburghe Club, 1928

Harting, H. M., *The Coming of Christianity to Anglo-Saxon England*. London: Batsford, 1971

Kendall, H. P., *A Short History of Whitby Abbey*. Whitby: Whitby Literary and Historical Society, 1969

Ker, W. P., *The Dark Ages*. London: Nelson, 1955

Mitford, Rupert Bruce-, *The Sutton Hoo Ship Burial*. London: British Museum Department of British and Mediaeval Antiquities, 1972

Patrick, Saint, *The Writings of St Patrick*. Tr. by N. J. D. White. London: S.P.C.K., 1932

Samson, Saint, *Life*. Ed. by Thomas Taylor. Oxford: U.P., 1925

Stenton, D. M., *English Society in the Early Middle Ages*. Pelican Books No. A 252 (1965)

Taylor, Thomas, *The Celtic Christianity of Cornwall*. London: Longmans, 1916

Williams, Hugh, *Christianity in Early Britain*. Oxford: Clarendon Press, 1912

Chapter 7. OUT OF THE DARKNESS

Asser, Joannes Menevensis, *Life of King Alfred*. Tr. by L. C. Jane. London: Chatto & Windus, 1926

Chadwick, N., *Celt and Saxon*. Cambridge: U.P., 1963

Clapham, A. W., *English Romanesque Architecture before the Conquest*. Oxford: Clarendon Press, 1930

Crouch, Marcus, *Canterbury*. London: Longman Young, 1970

Deanesly, Margaret, *The Pre-Conquest Church in England*. London: Black, 1961

———, *Sidelights on the Anglo-Saxon Church*. London: Black, 1962

Earle, John, *The Alfred Jewel*. Oxford: Clarendon Press, 1901

Felix, *Life of St Guthlac of Crowland*. Tr. by C. W. Jones. Ithaca, N.Y.: Cornell U.P., 1947

Hodgkin, R. H., *History of the Anglo-Saxons*. London: O.U.P., 1953

Hugo, Thomas, *History of Athelney Abbey*. Somerset Archaeological and Natural History Society. *Proceedings*, xliii (1894)

Liebermann, Felix, *Die Heiligen Englands*. Hannover: Hahn, 1889

Mitford, R. L. Bruce-, *Saxon Rendlesham*. Proceedings of the Suffolk Archaeological and Natural History Society, xxiv (1948)

Morris, John, *The Age of Arthur*. London: Weidenfeld & Nicolson, 1975

Palliser, David and Mary, *York as They Saw it*. London: Sessions, 1979

Sawyer, P. H., *The Age of the Vikings*. London: Arnold, 1971

———, *From Roman Britain to Norman England*. London: Methuen, 1976

Wall, J. C., *Alfred the Great: His Abbeys at Hyde and Athelney*. London: E. Stock, 1900

Winchester, The Antiquities. Winchester: privately printed, 1850

Winchester, The City. Official Guide. Cheltenham & London: J. Burrow & Co., 1956

Wantage and District. Cheltenham: Manderley Press, 1968

EPILOGUE

The Anglo-Saxon Chronicle. Tr. by Benjamin Thorpe. London: Longmans, Green, 1861

The Domesday Book. Tr. by John Morris. Chichester: Phillimore, 1975

Nennius, *The History of the Britons*. Tr. by J. A. Giles. London: J. Bohn, 1841

INDEX

abbeys, *see* monasteries
Abelard, Peter, 96
Aethelfrith, King, 155
Aidan, St, 117, 120, 121, 122
Alban, St, 77–8
Alcuin (Ealhwine), 156
Alfred the Great, 92, 124, 125–6, 141–50, *142*, 152–3
Angles, 92, 112–14, 124, *see also* Saxons; York
Anglesey, 72–3
Anglo-Saxon Chronicle, The, 92, 144–5, 161, 162
animism, 70–2, 80, 85–6
aqueducts, *see* Dolaucothi
Arthur (Arturius), 92, 93, 95, 98, 107, 111–12, 143
Athelney, Somerset, 145, 149–50
Athelstan, King 36, 141
Augustine, St, 115–16, 124, 126, 127, 128
Aurelianus, Ambrosius, 93, 98, 111
Aurelius Mausaeus Carausius, M., 'Emperor of Britain', 60
Ausonius, Decimus Magnus, 40–3, 53–4
Avienus, *Ora Maritima*, 20
Avon, *see* Bath

barrows, *see* burial mounds
Bath, Avon, xvii, 81–4, *82*
battles: Chester, 155; Edington (AD 878), 145; Hastings (AD 1066), 157; Hatfield Chase (AD 633), 125; Menai Straits (AD 61), 72; Mount Badon (Mons Badonicus), 92, 112; Stamford Bridge (AD 1066), 157
Bayeux Tapestry, 157, *158*, 160
Becket, St Thomas à, 127–8
Bede, 77–8, 92, 95, 99, 103–4, 116, 126, 127, 133, 134–5, 140, 155, 159
Beowulf, 113–14, 164
Berhtwald, St, 127
Berin, 117
Bertha, Queen, 116, 126, 128
Bitterne, Hampshire (Glausentum), 62
Boadicea (Boudicca), 46, 56, 58–9
Borlase, Dr William, 15–16
Bosham, Sussex, 157–60
Brigid, St, 123
brochs, 17, 19
burial mounds, 34–6; *see also* Sutton Hoo

Caedmon, 133, 134–5, 136
Caerleon, South Wales, 55, 64
Caesar, Julius, 5, 6, 10, 45, 50, 72
Cambridgeshire, *see* Water Newton
Camden, William, xviii, *166*
camps, military, 65
Candida Casa, Scotland, 103–5
Canterbury, Kent (Durovernum), 126–8, 132
Canute, King, 149, 158, 159–60
Carmarthenshire, *see* Dolaucothi
Carn Brea, Cornwall, xx, 14–16, 39
Carn Euny, Cornwall 39
Carthaginians, 4, 20–30; *see also* Phoenicians; St Michael's Mount; Scilly Islands
Cassiterides, 20–30; *see also* Scilly Islands
castles: Castle-an-Dinas, Cornwall,

castles – *continued*
39; Colchester, 55; Cromwell's, Tresco *35*; King's Manor, York, 157; Montgomery, 151; Portchester, Hampshire (Portus Adurni), 60–2, *61*; St Michael's Mount, 31; Tintagel, Cornwall, 109; York Minster, 157
Cawston, Norfolk, 124
chapels, 95, 104, 107, 109; *see also* Lullingstone
Charles I, 123
Chaucer, 128
Chedworth, 75
Chelsea, London Borough of, 162, *163*
Chichester, Sussex (Noviomagus), 157
Christianity, 6, 67, 69, 71, 74–81, 93–4, 98, 103, 114–26, 131–2, 156; *see also* Alfred the Great; Canterbury; churches; hermits; Lullingstone; monasteries; Offa, King of Mercia; *and under individual saints*
churches, 90, 106, 107, 148–9; *see also* Candida Casa; Holy Trinity Church; St Martin's Church
Claudius, Emperor, 50, 55–56
Coelestius, 48, 49
Cogidubnus, King Tiberius Claudius, 50
Colchester, Essex (Camulodunum), 55–9
Colman of Kilmacdaugh, St, 112
Colman of Lindisfarne, St, 112, 120–2, 134
Columba, St, 121, 122
Conan, St, 95
Constantine the Great, 59, 75, 80
Cook, James, 7, 136
Cornwall, 9–10, 27, 95, 111, 123; *see also* Carn Brea; Carn Euny; castles; St Michael's Mount; Tintagel; Truro
Cranmer, Thomas, 127
Cromwell, Oliver, 33, 123
Crowland, East Anglia, 139
Cumbria, *see* Vercovicium
'curse tablets', 81
Cymbeline, King, (Cunobelinus), 55

Danes (Norsemen/Vikings), 127, 134, 143–4, 149, 150, 159, 164; *see also* Guthrum, King of the Danes; York
David, St, 95, 96, 105, 107, 117, 123
Deusdedit, St, 127
Devon, *see* Stannary Courts
Dicul, 159
Diocletian, Emperor, 60, 77
Diodorus Siculus, 27, 28, 29, 30, 31, 38, 64
Dion Cassius, 58
Dolaucothi, Carmarthenshire, xx, 51–2, 62–5, *63*
Domesday Book, xx-xxi, 161–4, *163*
Dorset, *see* castles; Hengistbury Head; Hinton St Mary
Druidism, 6, 15–16, 50, 70, 72–3
'Dykes, The' *see* Hengistbury Head

earthworks, *see* Canute, King; Hengistbury Head
East Anglia, 117, 119, 141, 145; *see also* Crowland; Ethelbald, King of East Anglia
Edwin, King of Northumbria, 116, 125
Egbert, Archbishop, 156
'Egyptian' bull (statuette), *37*, 38–9
Eric Bloodaxe, 156
Essex, *see* Colchester; Mucking
Ethelbald, King of East Anglia, 137, 140
Ethelbert, King of Kent, 115–16, 126, 128, 131–2
Ethelburga, 116

Facilis, Marcus Favonius (statue), 56, *57*
farmsteads, *see* Jarlshof
Fastidius, 47, 52–3

Fergus, King of Scotland, 141
Fishbourne, Sussex, 50
Flat Holme Island, 78, 95
forts, *see* Carn Brea; castles; Hengistbury Head; Jarlshof; Maiden Castle; Sron an Duin; Vercovicium
Frampton, Gloucestershire, 75
Frisians, 92

Gately, Norfolk, 124
Geoffrey of Monmouth, *Historia Britonum*, 110–12
Germain (Germanus) of Auxerre, St, 77, 97–8, 114–15
Gibbon, Edward, *Decline and Fall of the Roman Empire*, 66, 93–4
Gildas, St, 77, 78–80, 91, 92, 94–6, 98, 105
Glamorgan, *see* Llantwit Major
Glastonbury, Somerset, 76
Gloucester, 161
Gloucestershire, *see* Frampton; Gloucester; Lydney Park
Godric the Hermit, 135–6
gods: Celtic, *see* gods, nature; nature, 70–2, 80; *see also* animism; Druidism; Matres, the; Sulis, Temple of; Roman, *68*, 80, 81; *see also* Mithraism; Saxon, 80–1; *see also* Wodenism; *see also* Christianity; mosaics
Gorlois, Duke of Cornwall, 110–11
Greeks, 4, 5–6, 20, 26; *see also* Diodorus Siculus; Dion Cassius; Posidonius; Ptolemy; Pytheas
Gregory I, Pope, 115, 116, 126–7; *Regula Pastoralis*, 143
Gudwal, St, 95
Guthlac, St, 137–40
Guthrum, King of the Danes, 145
Gwen, St, 107–9

Hadrian, Emperor, 74–5, 100–1
Hadrian's Wall, xx, 71, 79, 80, 100–3, *100*, *101*, 111, 151, 153
Hafdan, 156
Hampshire, *see* Bitterne; Portchester; Winchester
Hanno, 23, 34
Harold, King, 156–7, *158*, 160
Hebrides, Outer, *see* Sron an Duin
Hengist, 98
Hengistbury Head, xx, 3, 4, 12–14, *12*, 18
Henry V, 33
Henry VIII, xvii, xviii, 123, 127, 136, 148, 149
hermits, 31, 93–6, 104, 123; *see also* Gildas, St; Godric the Hermit; Guthlac, St; Illtud, St; Michael, St
Hermit's Song, The, 137
Hertfordshire, *see* Welwyn
Hilda, St, 133–4, 136
hillforts, *see* forts
Himilco, 20–2, 34; *see also* Carthaginians
Hinton St Mary, Dorset, 75
Holy Trinity Church, Bosham, 157–60, *158*
Honorius, St, 126
Horsa, 98
Housesteads, *see* Vercovicium
Hyde Abbey, 148

Ictis, *see* St Michael's Mount
Igerna, 110–11
Illtud, St, 96, 105–6, 117
Iona, 122, 123
Ireland (Ivernia), 6, 10, 51, 122–3

Jarlshof, Shetland Islands, 16–19, *17*
Jerome, St, 48
Joseph of Arimathaea, 76
Josephus, 4–5
Justus, St, 126
Jutes, 92, 112–14, 124; *see also* Saxons

Kent, 119, 141; *see also* Canterbury; Ethelbert, King of Kent; Lullingstone

'King Alfred's Jewel', 150

Laud, William, 127
Laurentius, St, 126
Leland, John, xvii–xviii, 109
Llantwit Major, Glamorgan, 105–6
London, *v*, 58, 59; *see also* Chelsea, London borough of; Justus, St; *and under* Mithraism
London airport, 80
Lucius, 'a king of Britain', 77
Lullingstone, Kent, 53, 75, 80–1, 87–90, *88*
Lydney Park, Gloucestershire, 71–2

Maiden Castle, Dorset, 4, *15*
maps of Britain, *xvi*, *xix*, 6; *see also* Ptolemy; Strabo
Matres, the, (sculpture), *67*
Mellitus, St, 126
Merlin, 111–12
Michael, St, 33
mines, *see* Carn Brea; cassiterides; Dolaucothi; St Michael's Mount; tin; Truro
Mingulay, *see* Sron an Duin
Mithraism, *v*, 66–70, 73–4, 80, *85*, 87, 90; Temple of Mithras, London, 66, 84–7
monasteries, 78, *82*, 94–6, 117–18, 120–3, 128, 138–9, 140, 144–5, 148, 159; *see also* Athelney; Candida Casa; Glastonbury; Llantwit Major; St Michael's Mount; Tintagel; Whitby
Montgomery, *see* Offa's Dyke
Mont St Michel, 33
mosaics, 47, 75, 80–1, 89
Mucking, Essex, 113
museums: Ashmolean museum, Oxford, 150; British Museum, 75, 131, 133; Colchester, 56; London Museum, 87; National Museum of Wales, Cardiff, 64; Red House Museum, Christchurch, 12–13, 14; Museum of the Royal Institution, Truro, 16, 36–9, *37*; York, 156
myths, 4, 5, 6–7, 20; *see also* Arthur; Geoffrey of Monmouth, *Historia Britonum*

Napoleonic wars, 60, 62
naval stations, *see* Portchester
Nectan, St, 95
Nennius, 92, 112, 165
Ninian, St, 103–5
Nodens, 71–2, 80
Norfolk, 124
Normans, xx, 55, 62, 134, 149, 151, 157; *see also* Canterbury; Domesday Book; William the Conqueror
Norsemen, *see* Danes
Northumbria, 114, 117, 119, 141; *see also* Edwin, King of Northumbria; Oswy, King of Northumbria; York

Offa, King of Mercia, 141, 151–3
Offa's Dyke, 151–3, *152*
Orcades, *see* Orkney Islands
Ordnance Survey of Ancient Britain, xx, 11
Ordnance Survey of Dark Age Britain, 95
Orkney Islands (Orcades), 6, 17
Oswy, King of Northumbria, 119–22, 125, 133, 134
Oxfordshire, *see* Wantage

Patrick, St, 96–7, 117, 123
Paulinus, St, 95, 116, 125
Pelagius, 47–9, 78
'Phoenician' artefacts, *37*, 38–9
Phoenicians, xx, 3, 4, 9, 20–39 (Ch. 2)
pilgrimages, 70, 71, 77, 83, 127–8
Plutarch, 25–6
Portchester, Hampshire, 60–2, *61*
ports, *see* trading posts
Posidonius, 1–2
Pot of Gold, The, 45

Pseudo-Aristotle, *On the Cosmos,* 1
Ptolemy, xix, 4, 6, 26
Pytheas, xviii, xix, 3–4, 5, 7–11, 12, 13, 18, 162

Raedwald, King of the East Angles, *see* Sutton Hoo
rėligions, 66–90 (Ch. 4); *see also* Christianity; Druidism; Mithraism; Wodenism
Rendlesham, 132, 133
Richard fitz Nigel, 161
Romans, xx, 5–7, 20, 25–7, 29, 31, 40–65 (Ch. 3), 66–90 (Ch. 4), 153–5; *see also* Arthur; Bosham; Caesar, Julius; Hadrian, Emperor; Hadrian's Wall; St Martin's Church; Strabo; Vercovicium; Vespasian, Emperor
Ruin of Britain, The, see Gildas, St
Ruin, The, 83–4
Rutilius Namatinaus, Claudius, 94, 97

St Albans (Verulamium), xx, 59; *see also* Alban, St
St Aubyn, Sir John, 32, 33
St Martin's Church, Canterbury, 126
St Mary's, Scilly Islands, 33, 35
St Michael's Mount, Cornwall (Ictis), xx, 23, 25, 27–33, *32*, 39
St Ninian's Cave, 104–5
'Samson Cross', 106
Samson, St, 95, 96, 105, 117
Samson, Scilly Islands, 35–6, 95
Saxons, 80, 91–2, 98–9, 112–16, 124–6, 127, 128, 141, 164; *see also* Alfred the Great; Bosham; Guthlac, St; Harold, King; Offa, King of Mercia; Oswy, King of Northumbria; Sutton Hoo; Whitby
Scilly Islands, 26–7, 33–6, *35*; *see also* Cassiterides; Samson
Scotland, 123, 141; *see also* Candida Casa; Jarlshof; Orkney Islands; Shetland Islands; Sron an Duin
Selsey, Sussex, 159
Shetland Islands (Thule?), 6, 9, 10, 18; *see also* Jarlshof
Shorne, Sir John, 124
Sidonius Apollinaris, 91
Silchester (Calleva Atrebatum), xx
Silvia, St, 47, 50n.
Simon of Sudbury, 127
Sir Gawain and the Green Knight, 164
Smythe, John, 159
Somerset, *see* Athelney; Glastonbury
Sron an Duin, Outer Hebrides, 11
Stannary Courts, 36
Stonehenge, xx, 72, *73*, 111
Strabo, 5, 10, 26
Suffield, Norfolk, 124
Suffolk, *see* Sutton Hoo; West Stow
Sulis, Temple of (Aquae Sulis), 81–4, *82*
Sussex, *see* Bosham; Chichester; Fishbourne; Hengistbury Head; Selsey
Sutton Hoo, Suffolk, 128–33, *129*, *130*

Tacitus, 40, 59–9, 72–3
Taranis (Wheel God), 71, 72
temples, 55–6, 58–9, *67*, 71–2, 80, 90, 116, 132–3; *see also* Sulis, Temple of; *and under* Mithraism
Tertullian, 76
Theodore, St, 127
Thule, *see* Shetland Islands
Timaeus, 2n., 9
tin, 9–10; *see also* mines
Tin Islands, *see* Cassiterides
Tintagel, Cornwall, 107–9, *108*
tombs, 54, 56, 104; *see also* burial mounds; Sutton Hoo
towers, *see brochs*
trading posts, *see* Hengistbury Head; St Michael's Mount
Tresco, Scilly Islands, *35*
Truro, Cornwall, *see under* museums
Tyler, Wat, 127

Uther Pendragon, King, 110–11

Venus (statuette), *68*
Vercovicium, Cumbria, 100–3, *100*
Vespasian, Emperor, 157–9
Vikings, *see* Danes
villas, 41, *41*, 43, 45–7, 72, 75, 83, 106, 157–9; *see also* Fishbourne; Lullingstone
Vortigern, King, 98

Wales, 123, 141; *see also* Anglesey; Caerleon; Dolaucothi; Llantwit Major; Offa's Dyke
wall paintings, 46, 75, *88*, 89
walls, Roman, 56–8, 59
Wantage, Oxfordshire, *142*, 149
Water Newton, Cambridgeshire, 75
Welwyn, Hertfordshire, 80
Wessex, 119, 145
West Stow, Suffolk, 113
Whitby, Yorkshire, 133–6, *135*; Synod of, 112, 119–23, 134
Whithorn, *see* Candida Casa
Wigtown, *see* Candida Casa
Wilfrid, Bishop of York, 120, 121–2
William of Malmesbury, 150
William the Conqueror, 157, 161, 164–5
William the Englishman, 127
William the Frenchman, 127
Winchester, Hampshire, 148, 149
Wodenism, 114, 116, 124, 151; *see also* Sutton Hoo

York (Eboracum/Eoforvic/Jervik), 141, 153–7, *154*, *155*
Yorkshire, *see* Whitby; York

Zosimus, 93–4